IOAN ES. POP

No Way Out of Hadesburg and Other Poems

Translated by
Adam J. Sorkin and Lidia Vianu

Featured Artist
Nicolae Aurel Alexi

University of Plymouth Press

20 ROMANIAN WRITERS SERIES

Ioan Es. Pop's *No Way Out of Hadesburg and other Poems* is the sixth title to be published in the series 20 Romanian Writers by the University of Plymouth Press. The series is one aspect of the University of Plymouth's ongoing commitment to introduce Romania's vibrant artistic culture to other nations. In addition to the literature, the University of Plymouth will be hosting a series of exhibitions and performances of Romania's visual and musical arts over the next five years. The following supplement features one of Romania's leading contemporary artists.

Featured Artist

NICOLAE AUREL ALEXI

Through his re-interpretation of classical styles, motifs and genres, Nicolae Alexi (born 1947) aims to give a lesson not only in technical mastery, but also in visual culture. His work is an incursion into the history of art, from the early Renaissance to the French eighteenth century. Rather than being didactic or exhaustive in nature, this is a humorous presentation of certain chapters in visual history, charged with subversive undercurrents of the erotic, the grotesque and the absurd. Alexi's stylistic designs are populated with a cast of strange and outlandish characters – often including the artist's self-portrait – with 'man' standing as an allegorical figure or protagonist in Alexi's meditations upon the drama of the human condition that complements Pop's suggestion that there might be 'no way out'. Charged by a fervent imagination, his artwork has drawn comparisons with the magic-realist prose of twentieth century Latin America.

Alexi is a graduate of the Nicolae Grigorescu school of Fine Arts. He was President of the Romanian Artists Union (1993-1999) and now works as Head of the MA Drawing Department at the National University of Arts, Bucharest.

Liz Wells

„Amintiri din viitor" Flexj '05

"foot-ball" Alexej 2005

IOAN ES. POP

No Way Out of Hadesburg and Other Poems

Translated by
Adam J. Sorkin and Lidia Vianu

Contents

Adam J. Sorkin

this is hadesburg and anywhere you run to will be hadesburg

Introducing Ioan Es. Pop

Ioan Es. Pop's first collection of poetry, *No Way Out of Hadesburg* (in Romanian, *Ieudul fără ieșire* – a title I'll comment on a bit later), appeared in 1994 in Bucharest from the prestigious Cartea Românească (The Romanian Book) publishing house. It was immediately recognised as an important book by critics and reviewers, who showered it with such praise as 'bizarre and deeply tragic,' 'profound – in a grave register,' 'dense,' 'grotesque,' and 'eloquent.' The Romanian Writers' Union awarded Pop its prize for a first book of poetry. As Pop's title suggests, it is a claustrophobic book, psychologically confined, about lives measured in 'years of/death, from... birth till now,' lives synonymous with the experience of the poetic persona whom, for convenience, I'll call by the author's name despite some distance between the two. Were it not at moments wry and surprising, though never bitter with the gall of the hopeless and sardonic, it might be called a dispiriting book as well, for it is full of dark truths illuminated by tragic assumptions about life.

No Way Out of Hadesburg – at least to this translator – is the product of a sympathetic imagination, the expression of a genial, compassionate sensibility. Pop's gift is for understated comedy rather than mordant protest at life or excoriation of human destiny. I suggest that this is true despite the centrality of the story about the death of Mircea, the speaker's double, with whom he lived in unbearable cold one long winter without wood for heating. The poet proclaims in a gesture of frank authenticity, 'i haven't wanted to write about anything else since.' Definitive of Pop's literary universe is that a Jesus shows up twice; once very much as an ordinary son of man, arriving 'in a dirty shirt, .../an empty bottle in one hand, staggering, crooning tra-la-la,' and at another point as a dirty beggar who at Christmas drags a cross, 'that stick of wood on his back,' throughout the city of Bucharest, 'a man more foolish and more down on his luck than we.' This drunken beggar, 'too much like us' either to dismiss or respect, perfectly illustrates the poetry's human empathy mixed with seriousness of purpose. Part of the reason is that Pop's style evokes a bedrock humanity beneath the anger and foregrounded experimentalism of much writing after the fall of communism in Romania. Reflected in a hallucinatory way, a mirage perhaps, the restrictions and severe deprivations of Romania's bleak 1980s, a period of widespread scarcity, strict censorship, and domestic terror, shadow Pop's pages as shared human limitations, existential, not special, circumstances. His style has nothing of the brittle surface of self-conscious ironies or verbal high jinks, or the petulant or plaintive, usually slangy speech of many of his disgruntled contemporaries for whom the new post-communist freedom of expression quickly ran a half-century's gamut of poetic liberations and formal fracturing (to echo the name of a movement of literary and ethical protest, the 'fracturists'), along with just about every possible rhetorical rebellion against self-restriction. Pop's aesthetic world, *mutatis mutandis*, is one of fundamental emotional and spiritual resistance to mortality, to fear, to human life in a seeming Kafkaesque world where 'the walls come closing in day by day' and life wears down or wears out, where home offers a patrimony of 'bright-eyed, ready-made/death.' The prodigal son may return, but, as in the last of the stop-action moments that make up the sequence, *A Life on One Single Day*, he brings 'carts heaped high with nothing, .../nobody will have as much nothing as we.'

Ioan Es. Pop was born March 27, 1958, in the village of Vărai, Maramureș, a province in the north of Romania. He graduated with a degree in Romanian literature and language from the University of Baia Mare in 1983, and was assigned to teach in the village of Ieud. After six years of teaching a variety of grade levels, he received hard-to-get permission to move to Bucharest, with the proviso that he work as an unskilled labourer at Nicolae Ceaușescu's monstrous edifice in the centre of Romania's capital, the 'House of the People' (first, though, he spent a month as a pig watcher for the chief engineer). Pop lived in Bucharest in dormitory-like housing for the unmarried, staying there until 1992; this experience is the source for this book's opening poem, which has as its title his address during those years, *No. 15 Olteț Street, Room 305*. At the time of the December 1989 revolution, the workers all laid down their tools and went in support of the protestors. In mid-January when they returned to work, construction at the site was suspended; Pop and his fellow workers were formed into groups to clean up buildings damaged during the protests. At the end of March, 1990, having been engaged as proofreader at a leading literary magazine, *The Evening Star* (*Luceafărul*), Pop was able to quit his job as a labourer. Although he had been writing poetry since the mid-1980s, there had been few opportunities for young authors under Romania's repressive policies, either to publish or to work in book publishing or journalism. Pop has continued to work in journalism for *Luceafărul* and other periodicals such as *PRO TV Magazine*. Today, he is editor-in-chief of *The Sunday Paper* (*Ziarul de duminică*), the cultural supplement of *The Financial Daily* (*Ziarul Financiar*), and also senior editor of the review, *Discovery* (*Descoperă*).

No Way Out of Hadesburg was soon followed by a second volume of poetry, *Porky* (*Porcec*, 1996 – the title is a made-up nickname based on the Romanian term for pig, 'porc', plus a Czech-sounding suffix), then a book of poems with an address as a title, *No. 113-bis Pantelimon Highway* (*Pantelimon 113 bis*, 1999), which won prizes from both the Romanian Academy and Writers' Union. Four years later, *Party on the Crosswalk* (*Petrecere de pietoni*, 2003) appeared and was awarded a Writers' Union prize as well as similar recognition from the rival Association of Professional Writers of Romania (ASPRO). The year after, Pop was granted the honorific Order of Merit from the Ministry of Culture. His other books include two bilingual collections published in Romania, *Rugăciunea de antracit/The Anthracite Prayer* (2002) and *Lumile livide/The Livid Worlds*, (2004), both with English translations by Nathaniel Smith, K. Shaver, and Ion Crețu. Pop also published a pair of volumes of selected poems, The *Attic-Bridge* (*Podul*, 2000 – this Romanian title means both things, so to keep the ambiguity the poet intended, I've yoked the English equivalents with a handy hyphen) and seven years later *No Exit* (2007), entitled with the English phrase. Pop also was featured in two collaborative volumes, *Confort 2 Renovated* (*Confort 2 îmbunătățit*, 2004, with Lucian Vasilescu – this is another impossible title, an estate agents term for a second-category dwelling, with the numeral suggesting the double authorship), and a book given as a title a metaphor from the last section of what I'd call the stop-action sequence, *A Life on One Single Day*, in this book, *A Cart Heaped High with Nothing* (*O căruță încărcată cu nimic*, 2008, with poets Peter Srager and Robert Șerban, a dual-language publication in Romanian/German). In 2009, Pop republished *Ieudul fără ieșire*. Currently he is working on a new book to be called *Tools for Sleep* (*Unelte de dormit*), to be probably publish in 2011.

No Way Out of Hadesburg and Other Poems consists of Pop's complete debut collection of 1994 translated for the first time in its entirety, plus another 11 poems that the author wanted to include in order to represent his later work. The first half dozen of these additional poems derive from Pop's 1996 *Porky* (*Porcec*). The next (*with these eyes that i've never seen with*) appeared in his 2006 volume of old and new poems in Romanian, *No Exit*. And the remaining four, the most recent in the book, are part of the manuscript of the as yet unfinished book of poetry I mentioned (the closing work, *beyond*, in fact refers to a change of mindset 20 years after the 1989 revolution that overthrew communism).

The title of this collection in English, *No Way Out of Hadesburg*, adapted a bit freely from Pop's first volume, gave the translators much occasion for thought. The latter two words of the Romanian title, 'fără ieșire,' can be rendered a number of different ways, some drab, others more allusive: 'without an exit,' 'lacking egress,' 'dead end,' 'blind alley,' 'cul-de-sac,' as well as the equally idiomatic but evocative Sartrean 'no exit.' I felt strongly that this last possibility seemed so obvious, with the poet himself having used it for a collection of original language poems, that it approached literary cliché. Finally, 'No Way Out' struck the translators as the best choice, three emphatic monosyllables, a turn of phrase in everyday speech that sounded right when combined with the English equivalent of the book's imaginary place (or no-place).

Though the name of an actual place, Ieud, the book's fictive locus, not so much physical as metaphysical, presented its own translation dilemma. In reality, Pop remarked to me with a touch of amusement at the disparity, Ieud is a pretty town, nothing like the way he makes it appear in the book. I myself know the region from a trip by car nearly thirty years ago, when my family and I drove through a gorgeous wooded terrain of mountains, valleys, and streams, visiting a number of unusual, historic wooden churches. Pop's appropriation of the village's name in fact occasioned a ludicrous protest from an outraged teacher there, as if the poet had written about the Ieud one could find on a map; the teacher threatened, if Pop dared to set foot in town again, he'd never leave. However, the book's Ieud has not only no way out but only a textual way in. The poetic space isn't even consistently coterminous with that of the town. As mentioned earlier, the opening sequence of poems refers to where the poet lived in Bucharest while he wrote the book, and the poet transplants other districts of Bucharest as well.

More to the purpose here, the name Ieud is a pun in Romanian, a near homonym for a common term for hell or Hades, 'iad.' It is this association which led the translators to interpret the place-name in English rather than, as is our usual practise, to use Romanian nomenclature as in 'borșa,' the 'dâmbovița' river, or the partially rendered 'big șomcuta,' carrying them over directly for the sake of specificity or perhaps, in some readers' perspectives, an exotic touch of elsewhere. Despite the connection to biographical data of the poet's life, the translation had to consider the pun as the paramount lexical feature of Pop's use of the village name in the title, so it became important to carry across for readers in English its not so hidden meaning. Hence (with a slight nod to Mark Twain), Hadesburg. Comments that Ioan Es. Pop made in a kind of interview consisting of a long written response to a literary journal's inquiry reinforce this decision: 'Ieud-Iad suits very well my conception of the world.' He went on, 'It is necessary to say, on the other hand, that Ieud, and also No. 15 Olteț Street and No. 113-bis Pantelimon Highway... are in spite of their exact reference to a real space, imaginary addresses.' Indeed, to Pop, not merely the represented world, also the poet embodied as a voice in his work, are verbal creations: 'The places, situations, and facts are 90% interior,' in a manner he termed 'demonised.' Pop conceived this process as involving the creation of both the text and the agent of the text. Poetry is the result, literally, of inspiration: 'above all in poetry, the author is not the author, he is only the instrument with which someone else writes, through which someone else breathes...'

In any case, the village of Ieud to be found on the book's pages is what I might call an arbitrary phonetic tag for a symbolic construct suggested by geographical and personal-historical happenstance, not an attempt at documentary verisimilitude – just as Ioan Es. Pop's middle initial (written so as to spell out the pronunciation of the letter-name 'S' in Romanian, the same pronunciation as in English) stands for nothing, an alphabetical contrivance to distinguish him from another poet with the same first and last names. Or so I thought until I asked Ioan, who, while agreeing that this was his intent, emailed me back that his adopting 'Es.' was not really accidental. As with Ieud, there was a biographical reason, two in fact, both representing powerful psychological factors. First, a student colleague he was in love with would call him 'Iohannes' (I hear 'Ioan Es.,' don't you?). And for the second, Pop added, he could hardly be unaware that the capital letter of his father's name was also 'S,' for Simion.

A couple of further remarks about translation decisions begin with the fact that this translation of Ioan Es. Pop pays attention to rhyme. His poems are not heavily rhymed, and the author in fact suggested to me that finding correlative rhymes in English was far from compulsory. Yet his style is neither flatly conversational nor colloquial in effect, just as his self-projection in his poetry is neither biographical in the sense of being limited to facts about the living Ioan Es. Pop nor revelatory in the sense of its being intimately confessional. Rather, despite Pop's inventiveness, absurdity, and illogic, details are raised to a dramatic intensity imbued with a ritual, indeed mythic quality in part through the repetitions, the verbal and imagistic rhythms, the internal echoes, the heightening readers expect of poetic discourse. The moments of rhyme are a sign of this highly charged lyric intensity. Also, Pop's sometimes prosy lines and prose-poem passages are concomitantly prose-like more or less as they are in the original; Pop told me in Bucharest in the summer of 2009 that his poems can be 'stories in disguise.' I took this to mean that his authorial confidence risks encompassing episodes that gravitate toward story-telling more than poetic music-making. Moreover, the translation preserves authorial idiosyncrasies such as words hyphenated at syllables at the end of some lines, small train-wrecks of words smashed together, or occasional broken-off, intentionally unfinished phrases (elliptical, but likewise puzzling).

Finally, one particular verbal formula demands comment, Pop's repeated use of the Romanian 'amic.' This informal, obviously Latin-derived term for 'friend' can't help but be seen in Romanian literary usage as characteristic of the eminent late nineteenth, early twentieth-century comic satirist in the theatre and in prose sketches and stories, I.L. Caragiale, whom Pop thus evokes by this gambit (this is but one of a number of allusions in Pop, which I won't take the time to go into). The word 'amic' plays an important role in *No Way Out of Hadesburg,* and the translation renders it in different ways as tone, grammar, and prose rhythm require, e.g., 'buddy' or 'pal,' or as an address, 'my friend' or 'good buddy,' and 'amigo' (this last I hear as an Americanism, one suggested by Pop's 'san-jose louse' that is used twice in the poem *No. 15 Olteţ Street, Room 305* – and the OED's examples of its use in English from mid-nineteenth century on back me up). 'The amigo' takes on a special prominence as the moniker for the drunken, despairing Bucharest beggar who winds up a suicide in the river but who proceeds to meet God, 'a runty little guy, mostly bald, cross-eyed.' It is hoped that these translation choices enhance the poems' richly metaphoric textual microcosm.

Within the poetry's bleak suggestion that life in the world is no more than life imprisoned in the local and universal hell of 'your own flesh. you can't take if off,' its sometimes psychotic and strange, sometimes homely and absurd imagery, its deep seriousness conjoined at one and the same time with a bittersweet, gently mocking black comedy, ultimately Hadesburg is everywhere and nowhere, 'boundless' – a psychological state. Pop's poetry offers *No Way Out of Hadesburg* as a kind of catharsis of pain and futility, where 'the end' takes refuge in the persona's apartment (only you take me in when i've no home), life is a progression of beds to a final one 'that has a lid,' and the dream self has to venture forth to assist in bearing its own body for burial ('your father's/already on his way to fetch you…/go help him lift you up, for/you've been lying there three days with no living breath'). Life and death seem both agony and a reciprocity of temporary anodynes: 'here/ life gets swigged down, death forgotten.' For Pop, however, this situation holds something inherently redemptive: 'I wrote somewhere that poetry is born together with prayer,' he stresses in the long, 'confessional' interview-response I quoted earlier, even when it 'begins to express doubts, fears, to criticise and to curse.' What must remain is the essential, the poetry itself living as the body of work of the author. Pop inverts this truism in typically skewed, zany fashion. To conclude, I'll borrow a striking metaphor from the poem *job. iova. jonah. ioan.* The speaker's friend, the mad, grouchy writer Iova, announces that an ultrasound has shown him the grave literally expanding inside him and goes on to imagine his future as the future of his written work. Similarly, Pop's poetry suggests that writing is the only thing that holds out the hope of transcending the impossibilities and limitations of mortality: 'one day…,' the poet taunts the world and its travail, 'i'll be a book bound in my own skin.'

NO WAY OUT OF HADESBURG

No. 15 Olteț Street, Room 305

1.
like a huge, bitter seabird
misfortune hovers over the block of flats
at no. 15 olteț street.

only those like us live in these rooms. no families. here
life gets swigged down, death forgotten.

and no one ever knows who or whom, who with
whom, when or what for.
sometimes the wind blows the smell of smoke and the tumult of battle
from the catalonian plain.

when you come up to see us, buddy, watch out: you'll be met at the
                    doorway by the san-
jose louse. he's our keeper. he'll wag his tail at your feet, he'll
greet you, hey, amigo, slip me five to ferry you across. the door's
always bolted, these guys keep locking me out, they imprison me outside.
don't believe *him*, pal, you've no idea. the janitor came yesterday
and made him chief of the landing, he's in charge of
this room now – this accursed ship the waters have tossed here,
marooned on the third floor.
pay him, my friend, he's the helmsman. he still rocks on his sea-legs
as in the old days when the ship leapt through the waves.

if he swears, listen piously: when he swears
he's really praying. as they all do here.
as you'll soon do.

only those like us live here.
life gets swigged down, death forgotten.

at rare intervals of contrition, of faith, inevitably at night,
the walls grow thin, stretch this way and that, reach higher,
as if a fluttering shroud draped over an unworldly body.

but nobody awakens and in the morning again the building is
a rumpled shirt out of the pockets of which we alone can leave,
only we.

only those like us live here.
life gets swigged down, death forgotten.

2. group photo

seated around the table after supper. maybe pensive. maybe just
exhausted. fallen to the floor, its shirt open – a
rotten peach – lascivious dancer of these nights.
first on the left – zoli. with a reddish beard propped
on his fist. an empty glass overturned half out of the picture. his eyes
blurred. maybe just exhausted. maybe pensive. behind him
you can see the turned-up collar of my coat, as
though a hood. i always forget: no one's watching us anymore.
i walk as if wrapped in someone i'm not.

on the right end – hans. he's *something*. he's
thirty-eight. he's pillowed his head on the table.
once he had money. he had theresa. he's thirty-eight.
the guy had a pal, the pal had
theresa, theresa had hans's money. hans has
pillowed his head on the table. the table wobbles, us along with him.
he was thirty-six at the time. now he has size ten boots. a new life, and
cirrhosis of the liver wait for him in bed. among us,
hans is the only accomplished man.

mitru: no work for a year. fit for apostleship.
found shelter here. this flophouse takes in anybody.
once had a wife and a home, but done with those.

smack in the middle sits the spider with a cross.
always moody, wrapped in a shroud of his own silk
as in a gentle halo of flame.
'day breaks, night falls again,' he says,
'and none of them will awaken to betray us.'

3. the ordeal

he says, look, says i've got this box of matches, lifted them the other night from my aunt. he says, i've lost my spider, can't be nowhere else, he says, 'cept in 305. keep your eyes peeled, he says, watch the entrance, whistle when he goes out, he says, he's you name it and then some, got long legs, goes about in nothing on, only underwear, he says, bowlegged, makes like some snotty big shot, speaks through his nose, boy, weaves them incredible shirts. he says, you know, i and my sister with him, you know, and all that jazz. seen 'er one day, seen 'er next day too. so i pay 'em a visit one night. she, he says, she's wearing the cat fur – and was she meowin'! the little bitch purred, too, he says, so i'd take 'er for a pussycat. and the guy next to 'er, in bed. then, he says, i pulled the clock down off the wall and banged hell's bells out of it till next morning. then they came around and found 'er there, washed 'er, dressed 'er to be a bride. you know, they said, you're hot for him, well, you got him. all your life, gonna be a spider's wife. all right, take the weirdo, take your monster home. and she reaches for him. but, no, the spider shillyshallies, don't want her, no, he's too young, no, he needs her ear, so he can weave bridal blouses in it.

(and einshtein went to see this lady, his friend since forever. einshtein was old now and in one ear and out the other. einshtein saw this spider, the lady friend had raised him since he was tiny, like her own child. he liked the spider, this einshtein did. they hit it off right away. poor lady, oh mama. she went to the kitchen to bring sweets to her distinguished guest. then the old humbug – he snatches the spider real quick, stuffs it in his mouth, and starts to chew it up.

then his lady friend comes back. dangling out of the corner of einshtein's mouth there's an unswallowed leg.

what's that, she asks. nothing, the tip of my moustache.

they never seen each other again after that. she couldn't never forgive him.)

4. the triumphal arch

here's what i'm going to do now: head back to olteț street.
it's friday night.
from friday to monday might as well not be alive.
hans gets mad and buys a bottle of surgical spirits
zoli gets mad and buys a bottle of surgical spirits
i get mad too and tell them why
and they tell me why. after that we dilute
everything with water and begin to feel happy.

they no longer say why, i no longer say anything.
from friday to monday nothing can be heard.
we each drink our share and begin to feel
less unhappy. less alive.

and till sunday night it's ok
it no longer matters whatever is or isn't.
hans goes to the window and zoli goes to the window, but
no ship appears sailing from corinth.
they say, not monday yet. i say, not monday yet.

so on olteț it's happiness again.
friday comes and from friday to monday
day night day our free time
and we belt out songs until the rooms rattle –
trusty old salts who hope one sunday they'll see
on the horizon, beyond on the blocks of flats in colentina,
the ship returning from corinth.

then on monday, when everyone's out, at last
the Son arrives to redeem us:
in a dirty shirt, eyes puffy from sleeplessness,
an empty bottle in one hand, staggering, crooning tra-la-tra-la,
he climbs the stairs to three-zero-five, reaches out his hand,
and begs: tie me to the mast so i can sleep a bit, my friend.

5. baptism

in the room there's a watch that hans feeds in secret.
go faster, he whispers, faster.
he bought a shirt and dressed it. he
washes it, changes its shirt, takes care of it like the apple of his eye.
the watch is a sluggard. it's put on weight, it's spread
across the table, the lazybones can't stand up any longer –
when it ticks it's like a bark.
in the room there's a watch that hans feeds in secret.

there's also a watermelon hans brought to this house when it was tiny
and hans thinks it's his baby.
uh oh, baby's ripe and red.
one day someone stabbed baby's belly with a knife.
a moan could be heard. baby's blood gushed out flavourful and sweet.
we were baptised in its coolness.

6.

we hired two guys from room 24. look, man,
they pray for us night and day, we'll be for-
given, no doubt about it. we can
keep drinking.

7.

four junipers with beards tour our block of flats.
the janitor chases them away with open scissors.
we're priests, they yell, nobody can cut our hair.
we're magi, you've no right.
for three months we've been travelling to his room
to see the miracle in three-hundred-five –
we're magi, you evil-smelling herod. we've come
to witness his birth and carry him to his tomb.

8. the hans bird

a bird flew in through the window at night
i knew for sure it was hans.
it was bald and dead drunk.
hey, he said, here's 50 *lei*, they've got
some kick-ass brandy across the road. *nevermore*, i replied.

he said: since i went away from you, they
hired me as night watchman at the cemetery. i have
a first-class flashing light. i sleep by day. i work with
the police. i've money enough to bury you. i've become minerva's
owl. i open my eyes only at nightfall.

they promoted me. i now have large epaulets
on my liver. i had them since the time
here with you. oh! my wounds remain sore.
get going, man, let's have a little something to celebrate.

hansi, i told him, *nevermore*.

9. zoli

who, you know, who among you's got a house and home elsewhere?
                    gooood,
let him leave us. man, you got parents? a girlfriend?
kids? would anyone adopt you? come on,
whoever it is, off you go. hansi,
man, you got a mother? scram. hey, folks, have you, you know, you got
anyone to pity you? bye-bye baby. boy, you, anyone miss you?
so long! you, there, ever been happy in your life? ciao.
see ya! vamoose.

hansi, you damn fool, that's the window, the door's over there.
come on, boy, up up up. it's three a.m. and happiness
will thump our butts if we don't beat it outa here.
line up, boy. off to work, boy. after me, boy,
step on it. from dawn to dusk, by the clock. come on, move
it, or happiness will wake us. hansi, my boy,
keep the hell away from her, boy,
many have died at her hand.

10.

i still think now i could have gone awry in a worse way
than how bad i really became.
and what happens today may be the same tomorrow,
the same yesterday. but the san-jose louse showed up,
pushed in belly first, hands behind his back,
speechified the whole day long. i asked, he answered, i found out
he'd been appointed emperor of no. 15 olteț street.

i clapped my hands. i carolled. it's a new age
at no. 15 olteț street. everybody's happy.
we've got long tongues in our boots and in our bells. as during
the time of *our* beloved gaddafi
who's in cuba and eats his vietnamese rice
out of korean sugarcane.

for tomorrow, we've been promised chloroform. tomorrow the world will
                     turn
more ethereal, more refined. it will waft from us
as through gauze.
it will be a lot more pleasant on the operating table.
even there, truth will hide behind our back.

they will remove from us only the outside world.
death will stay intact inside us.
life will stay exact inside us.

from tomorrow on, we promise to stop drinking,
stop making trouble in the block,
stop using the sceptic system.
from tomorrow on, we promise to stop drinking.

but tomorrow is another today – what a disappointment!
tomorrow will never be tomorrow.

No Way Out of Hadesburg (I)

1. in hadesburg with no way out. once we were there, too.
we're there now, we'll be there tomorrow and the day after,
and forever the water of the same river will bathe us.

how many months has it been just night and day,
how many months have we searched everywhere for him?

pay heed, passerby: space there
suddenly veers to the left, the reptile's head
gets severed from its body, the plaster of the neck cracks, breaks.

on its own, the head floats across dry land and water,
solitary, the only thing there on
sebastian's ship.
pay heed: if you stray into that place,
no map will be of use.

in vain you'll struggle to find your way out, in, out,
in vain you'll want to tear the shroud of the space
you've strayed into. beyond, you'll find only
the traces of your own footsteps from here.
boundless, this hell of hadesburg, and there's no way out.

no geography has ever managed to come close to it.
no halo foretells it.
no comet's tail trails after.

like a cloud high in the heavens it floats across
dry land and water, no halo foretells it, no
comet's tail trails after.

2. composition written by ilea, ioana, pupil in fifth grade 'B'

the schoolteacher is talking to her fourth graders. children,
where is hadesburg and we said we never left it so how
can we know where it is. she said at least you have the train
we said the bus comes daily twice
a week via borşa on fridays she
sighed we laughed we said we would come visit
her flat that day and bring flowers we did
we left them in the middle of the room she stood in
the middle of the room with an open umbrella a
suitcase in one hand we asked what do you want to do
  she said i'm waiting for the bus
  i'm waiting for the bus
what bus do you mean what bus are you waiting for
in this room with no door and no window –
and she said this isn't a room children this is a street
except it's night here

what night it's not night you have dark glasses on
that's why you no longer can see us
and how could you leave us so soon, dear teacher, it's the beginning of
    november
the birds have begun to fade to yellow and fall
and the bus comes on friday and today is only tuesday,
then tomorrow, the day after, too, only tuesday, and when the bus
comes on friday, it comes via borşa.

3. i asked mircea, i said, mircea, wall up this
window, nobody lives here.
go ahead, fill it with bricks and mortar, or one day
it will lure me out.
i can't always cower under it.
but mircea said alas, people said alas, i said
alas, i meant to lend you this tea kettle long ago
to wear on your head when you walk from room to room.
it will be your helmet gleaming under the rays of night.

and here's the pointer i use to teach spain in geography.
make it your spear of glory –
arise and set forth into battle, thrust it
into your own boots until blood fills them from
the belly of our wooden horse.
tear down the granada of our bathtub, kill
the butterfly on the lamp. it's the monster that pillages
the sun in our toilet –

cordoba lies in the kitchen, the mice of doubt have
taken refuge there. kill doubt. we've lived with them too long
to know who's hunting whom.
our clothes aren't ours; by means of their innate power
they flutter in despair. go ahead,
make haste against the la mancha of our clothes,
thrust your spear into them and rid them of us.
you alone have lived all your life in
the spain of this room.
only you know how to.

4. i seldom go out and when i do the walls tremble, completely exhausted
by the effort of expulsion. one day
they will lack enough force to
push the foetus out.

here only the bed preserves a hint of human warmth.
i sleep, sink into the mattress, it
swallows me more and more,
my shoulders, nape, chest.

i sleep because tomorrow's coming
and i must sleep tomorrow too, within the clamshell of the pillow
it no longer matters whether i am me or i –
the mattress swells, gradually engulfs me
in its sweet darkness, hopeless, sightless,
then closes above me and is sealed by warmth like an envelope,
the sheet a placenta that scarcely allows breathing,

and mircea screams, wake up, but i no longer hear him.
wake up, he says, but i don't.
why should i, and what could i call mine
if i fully woke up?

5. one day we're awakened and hardly know who we are
and we say why and they say soon you'll have
your first hearing. you must be prepared to speak.
be very careful what you say, whatever you say in court will be
held against you. this is hadesburg and anywhere you
run to will be hadesburg.

6. the two of us were born mixed together, stuck
to one another, stuffed in the sack of the very same body,
powerless to disentangle from each other.

so people wouldn't say she only half made us
she never told us that we were two.
she told me you are the belly and the legs
she told mircea you are the head and the chest take care
you don't somehow forget your legs.

she never spoke to us in the plural as *you both*
she wrapped us together in the same coat.
i learned over time to be leg and hand
and he – just breath, just head.

till we realised we'd never met
till we realised that we were two
we'd no idea how well we'd been stuck to one another.
we couldn't see it before about twenty-five or twenty-six
when we met the first time.

i asked, are you mircea? he said, yes, my liege lord.
i said, *that*, you're not. he said, let's drink a
cognac and warm our-
selves. we had a beer. it was our
first discovery. he said, we're alike, or we wouldn't both
have beer. i said, we're like two peas in a pod, and if i be mistaken,
not a seed will sprout next spring,

we really were the same. his clothes were for half
a man, my clothes were for half
a man. we said, let's combine your cap with
my scarf, shirt with boots –
it'll be another occasion to toast one another.

he said, let's drink one more cognac. we boozed it up
that day. that night we

drank only water. we'd drunk
a cognac a day a month a year until.

finally one of us said he must be off,
there'd never be another bus.
the devil knows who stayed and who didn't
when mircea left.

7. we bang on the doors with our fists to let us
out, but whoever's out there can't hear us and
thcy'rc also banging on thc doors to bc lct in.
when the doors are finally opened, we find ourselves
but don't recognise ourselves, and we say we want out.
they say we want in, don't take the door away,
what will we unlock when we go out?
only a hole in the wall will remain.
we won't have any way to go out.

8. i never once dared cry out. brother of
the mouse and the death-watch beetle gnawing in the dark from below
patiently and silently into the sole of the foot and upward to the knee,
as they learned from long generations of rodents
always forgotten in the cellars of the species.

we had no other honours. in the cold fable
we went unmentioned.
he who came trumpeting victory, punching his way,
knocking over corpses, never knew
it was we who gnawed at the root, we at the core, and he merely
pushed the surface a little from above,
hardly aided in the fall.

brother of the mouse and the death-watch beetle, we're again under
the newcomer's foot
together with the body inside which we gnawed and from
which we'd never yet managed to leave.

slowly, from underneath, in the dark, into the sole of his foot,
into the knee, we climb again, with the perseverance
we learned from
long generations of rodents.

when he begins to sense us, we're already in his belly,
patiently we've climbed to his chest –
little rodent principles, just as we'd been placed
directly below, at the root,
gnawing there patiently, gnawing very patiently.

9. on the fourteenth, i mean tuesday, i mean yesterday,
my life calculated it had reached its limit. my eyelids
became leaden. at my knees, as if at a railroad station, the train
of the femurs came to a stop. the hands clasped, then sidled
up the neck. they whispered something
in the ear, deliberated, climbed down for good
to eternal sleep in gloves.

let gloves be rooms for eternity
for my sad, thin, icy hands. my mouth has
withered as well. it said, you've kept yourself buried
so long in this cheek at the service of
your unnatural smile. adios, darling, i'm off
to sleep under the tongue. by my lonesome.

with you, even your shirt can't stay
happy. its silk is ruined
by the mouse gnawing at your bones.

but your shoes continue to be properly black. they will
mourn your toes. they will mourn you.
a toenail will be priest, the knees the band of musicians,
the shoulders godfathers, the hands wedding guests,

and the phosphorus in your fingernails the candle leading the cortege.

10. when i'm happy – and that happens
more and more often, though really almost never –
the elements in the body long to reconcile, for a single night:
iron-isaiah dances, magnesium-peter sizzles
cold dark halos in the air
where one of a kind in a violet shroud
phosphorus-jesus ascends.
then my fingers emerge from their gloves dripping with ardour
like little girls from bathtubs:
my boots start reviling their soles, the mourners,
so i tug on their tongues but always remember too late
what japes my feet will in turn pull on me.

mircea, i say, if that's so, it's a sign we're alike.
we're like peas in a pod, he says, and if i be mistaken,
not a seed will sprout next spring,
the day splinters, his boots whisper anew
in some foreign lingo.
they will surely betray him one day and leave him
on his own at the mercy of feet that have
been unfaithful to him for a long time.

i haven't known a woman in a long time, he says.
but i like to watch the legs seek each other out
in the evening after they haven't
seen each other all day.
the soles draw near full of pity and
weep on one another's shoulder. i can't let them
meet very often, for i might lose them.
i keep them in separate boots,
when evening comes they can hardly wait for night.

i put them to sleep side by side. the toes chatter away, they make signs,
                    they say,
let him fall asleep first, we'll meet on his chest
(the fingers of those sexagenarian
hands, bigoted and smug,

have grown old coupling
in his shabby pockets).

well, mircea says, i wanted these legs
educated at a top boarding school. i
taught them all kinds of refined skills. i
made them out of the most elegant shoe leather.

(but his left hand had begun to act strangely:
it kept stealing out of his pockets and then at night
it mounted his chest to couple with the other.
in the morning it was difficult to wake them and chase them back,
one to his right, another to his left –
he felt cheated down to his fingernails.
i don't know why he didn't shoo them
to his fingertips, to live like apostles.)

lord, he still had so much life in him!
plenty enough to die.
i said, send those hands to a sanatorium somewhere.
they'll cut your throat one night.

but he kept delaying. first he had to teach them
to walk upright on their own,
as if those hands could be educated any more.
they were wrinkled due to the lead in books
and looked sexagenarian.

we might say he'd rather have gone blind than see himself cheated
and be called a sucker.

we might say what replaced them in his memory of cotton-wool
was a woman who was real.

to him, matter became mild, soft, generous
like a wool sweater that retained the woman's heartrending nonexistence
and hugged him inside in an endless embrace.

we might say every part of him, veins, bones, lungs,
formed corridors through which his breath
raced to meet her.

so it was. hell broke loose: the blind man consented to see once more.
and every part of him abandoned him. the lung refused him
and whispered to his glottis that breath should be a stranger.
his veins clotted. he never met her again.
his cough joined his lung at dinner.
in short, after that winter, on june 15, what happened to him happened
(you'll find out in the poem 'winter with mircea').
on september 15 the people at the inspectorate knew it, too.

11. my family made sure i never knew time.
even when i was twenty-six, they'd still bring me dolls to love.
they'd fill the room with dolls from their days, or their grandmothers':
every doll had stayed young and beautiful.

they claimed they were girls meant for me. i was to love only them.
so that time couldn't somehow find its way in. so that
i'd never escape into thirty.

each year they told me, today's your birthday, you're twenty.
the dolls, too, were always twenty. and they told me if you don't
go out, you'll always be twenty.
whenever i did go out, they'd hardly know me afterwards. everything
about me had shrivelled, had aged.
they were scared to death, they said; your dolls won't
recognise you, won't love you anymore,
you'll never win them back.
you can't go out. the weather outside is far too cold for.
your body is more delicate than.

your body can barely sustain a minimal existence
in which time's breath can almost not be heard.

12. he celebrates his birthday, he's happy. on
the table, candles, plates, glasses.
he's happy. he's lived thirty years of
death, from his birth till now.

13. since tonight is our birthday, we're allowed
to drink and celebrate, my dear friends.
here in your house tonight you have two among the many
who've lost everything – but tonight
have the servants lay the table as in the good old days,

call for flies in their knickers to fetch the aromas of grilled meat
from the feasts of the rich,
call for the angel of our house, the full-bellied death-watch beetle,
who at its leisure gnawed away our home and hope,
and let him be sommelier just for us: he should pour the thick wine
from the vatican cellars. for we're
important guests now, me and my pal. we pay like kings.
as we've paid for as long as we've lived.

and we can have something more, we can finish first in the
formula-one tragedy circuits. we've only a short
lap left:
our boots, our gala phaetons
stand ready in the passageway, under the portico.
we have until the sun on your ceiling rises –
when our coursers, our judas, our
iscariot feet have taken a rest.

and then call for more, order the principles that
stand upright in the telegraph poles: give us
a snappy military salute with your hand,
salute us as two who in the nights of yore
could have been saints or prophets. but who now
have nothing, no one to preach or prophesise to in the desert,
who are followed by a poor flock of devout rags –

help them, my precious: we've a few coins left from hope
that we no longer need. give them the change
so they may hope that one day they'll become
fine new clothes again.

14. flee from her flesh for it is dream flesh.
turn back to the hermitage of the body and try never
to abandon it again. bow low in the candlelight and leaf through
the once burning manuscript of walls,
but do not go beyond the pages that form
the stones in the walls. and from now on let
sleep overwhelm you.

when you have time on your hands bring mortar and bricks,
double the thickness of the walls, lower the ceilings
until there's no room left
except for sleep. and even more,
fill in whatever had been window or door.

do not apply words anywhere. words can
corrode lime and eat away the stones of a wall:
she will be there again on the other side.

flee from her flesh for it is dream flesh.

15. what mircea said to his disciples on november 10

today i'm not going home. but i know my fate:
one of you will awaken me.
one of you will betray me.
doctor dumitru will arrive too late.

for i am old, withered like the cold flowering
            of frost, shrivelled,
beaten by the sun for hours, overpowered by heat. winds have
            turned me black, roads
wearied me, days worn me away, years left me old,
            nights crippled, broken me –
and, worst of all, luck forsaken me.

glory, glory! here we stand before the gates of the orient.

where anything's possible, for
nothing's of use anymore.

16. only the dead on the battlefield are the victors here.
here everything started on a tuesday. yesterday
was tuesday. wednesday and thursday are also tuesday. tomorrow
comes and it's tuesday too. everlasting celebration.
the soul stands on tiptoe to see what day
stretches beyond the horizon. such quivers of joy for
it's another tuesday.

where did this midnight find them?

a withered rose as a boutonnière, each of them went down to
his own ithaca,
each prised open the putty jaws with effort,
each entered with great difficulty.

glory, they shouted. glory, they intoned. glory, they whispered.
glory to the room that swallowed us,
the twilight of the gods has found us
unprepared, waiting for mircea
whoneverturnedup.

has he risen?

with fifes and stone trumpets.
but no one could see:
gushing forth from a mouth
shining bright as olympus –
with no way out
of
    h
      a
        d
          e
            s
              b
                u
                  r
                    g.

Winter with Mircea

in this winter loneliness i no longer have the courage
to make a fire in the fireplace as it gives off
much more smoke than fire

in this provisional happiness from
november through march
i know tomorrow won't be like yesterday but
like today and today and today always today
and from today to today nothing much can get done.

it's true in this loneliness no solitary man could
last long. but a heavy burden of
trifles have to be attended to:
the urge to live at all costs
the incapacity to love anymore and
yesterday.

had you known mircea you'd have understood.
understood what? i myself understood too late.
we lived together for a year in the same flat, and
that winter without wood we slept at minus 14 degrees.
i haven't wanted to write about anything else since.

in autumn we didn't give a damn where we had to live.
but then he developed lung problems.
we stayed there that winter without wood. it
was a bitterly cold winter
when we stayed together all winter without wood.

they said we drank and that was why we didn't,
of course, why we didn't, yes, didn't meet our obligations.
he had something in the chest and then
spring came and he continued to
cough and i said

we should stop drinking and stop being.
but he said maybe reading had exhausted him,
and they said we must be crazy if we didn't
understand that we must.

and mircea stood with his head bowed and
kept silent the whole time and i
kept silent the whole time and they thought we wanted to defy them
and mircea died in june, we
heard about it in september when he didn't

return to the job. then our flat became mine,
merely mine, the entire next winter
they said, see, mr pop, you have
a flat now. you have all the privileges. someday
soon you'll be a regular teacher and have
a ten-day vacation at christmas and the new year. but
after that please come back to buy
wood for the fire. after all it's your business to.
in summer you'll have no vacation if you take
the time now, you're still
a teacher on probation, not a good idea to.

remember mircea zubaşcu last year, he used up
his time off during the winter holiday and then had none left for the summer holiday. see, he died, for
instance, we can let the inspectorate know.

they told him comrade zubaşcu we want you not to leave
our locality on saturdays. he had a
girl in borşa. she thought he'd marry her. she
loved him so much. saturday

was training day, he had no classes. don't
leave town, study on your

own, come to school at eight to support our training committee. he came for about

three weeks in a row but then he
left friday night until monday morning,
and they got so awfully worried.
i didn't know him very well myself back then.

then the two of us lived together, she
came, shesawwehadnowoodandleft,
so he followed her to try to convince her we didn't, no, didn't
drink, and she probably couldn't understand.

he returned and we spent all winter at
minus, she never came again, he
invited me to drink a cognac to warm ourselves,
then i invited him to drink a
cognac to warm ourselves,
that winter he began coughing
blood and wouldn't go to

a doctor, spring came he
continued to cough, and she never
visited us again. the spring warm-
up began. when he went to see her the last time, she

had somebody else. he came back,
stayed a few more days, left again
at six in the evening without saying a word. when i
went to his burial and i saw
them carry him to the grave, i said, tomorrow,
i have to go back to school. i had to get my lesson plans done. i didn't see her when he
was buried. she was at borșa. she was
making her lesson plans for the next day.

when they said what they said we listened
and did what they said but then again we didn't
do what they said, after that they told us not
to again but we did again.

when they sent us to live in the flat,
we went and lived in the flat,
we said we'd live in the flat,
it wouldn't be a problem, but

we spent six months in the flat,
we lived two months in the flat at minus 14,
they didn't know, they said
they didn't, and we didn't, and our interest despite,

it's no excuse, we'd better not, as maybe
nobody would tell about, and when we did what they said,
we didn't do what they said, and he in june, we found out
only in september, on september 15.

No Way Out of Hadesburg (II)

1. do you really believe we are no more than we are this moment
at the table or in our gestures when sober or as we jostle
every morning at the newsstand or on long autumn evenings
when we return home always the same way with the very same movements
along streets always the same?

those who live tomorrow won't ask themselves this question.
but we, here and now, isolated from the language that will bring things to
                              a close,
have dug our fingernails into plaster and scratched in vain, have stood
                              pressed against the walls
in vain: nothing could be heard from beyond –
at the dead end of our speech no answer has yet been spelled out.

only once in a great while have we opened our eyes. then we
saw heaps of the unknown thrown upon us
as upon coffins, so at once we closed them again
and quickly said, it's not true, we're still alive, i'm alive, he's alive,
he's alive – i touched the one lying beside me.
he's alive – he tossed in his sleep, laughed, sighed.

do you really believe we were heard in no other room
that we hadn't time to enter?
or that the room wasn't yet walled up, or nobody lived in it yet,
or those who will live in it would come too late, or
they were there but never heard when we banged on the walls, or others
banged on the walls too at the same time and only they were heard,

or we failed to notice when we left one room for another,
one cellar for another, or refused out of fear to break down the walls
of the last room, or failed to imagine that beyond
the cellar there might be more rooms otherwise lit except for
ashes sifting in through the cracks in the back door,
or the front doors had not yet been installed into the walls and no other
room beyond that had yet been built? –

then we rushed back greedily upon our own bodies,
we climbed down and in a fury closed the trap doors above –
in a fury as if in a province of self-forgetfulness,
as if in a woman's womb we weren't meant ever to leave.

at least had we done this much: understood the question's failure.
then the owners of the bridge no longer would have unconditional power
           over
our bodies nor would our mistresses of whitewash,
neither the all but unstoppable cold nor the inarticulate blizzard
that chokes us, nor the walls gouged by our nails.

we allowed our body to swell above us,
to swell and flood,
to fill the rooms we lived in,
to leave no crack unfilled other than
the narrow stalk of our breath – auntie,

dear auntie, we've taken sick in the orient, send us money, we need money doctors medicines,
or in three months we'll find the only cure, we'll go meet the devil,
           auntie –
money, money, or we'll suffocate in this room, we need
another language here, we know it too well – ceiling walls floor –
outside, nothing can be seen through the windows,
outside, the beginning of no other speech
can be heard.

2. let him alone, i could hardly find him. he stole in there
at the first light of dawn and curled up under a plastic bag,
his eyes ruined from having kept them inside too long.
it's not his fault he can't talk.
he never knew a day when i took him out. he curled up,
whimpered, squeezed his eyes shut as if a beast had
leapt at his face. let him sleep, at least he won't howl the whole night,
won't scratch the walls with his nails. it's pointless
to wake him, speech won't do him any good.

stop, you worry too much. your daughter elvira is innocent, he said.
every day she did the shopping. this year her fingers have budded again,
in may we'll have chrysanthemums once more –
i won't let them wither like last year.
i'll cut them early, he said

elvira has come in. watch out, she told him, last night two men
went to the docks, they asked about you. i said i'd found you last year
in the abyss, your body pecked clean by birds
and your bones scattered – they went off, rest in peace. they
went away last night. my broth wasn't very good. i added
too little quicksilver to it. it slipped
asquickasawinkintoyourstomach and may you rest,

may you rest in peace, our dear father, may the earth lie gently.
now we have a flat. we have a child. we have five thousand *lei* of debt.
we have elephantiasis. we have an uncle who works in the ministry, he's my
                cousin,
he's read leopardi he's read the leopard. he can't see, can't hear, he's
my brother. he told me, may you rest in peace, it's started, it's coming this
                way,
the realm of psalms is beginning even now:
       upon you, oh my lord, the walls of my body have laid their foundation.
       you are the absence that i protect, you – the sleep that i sleep:
       if i am your heaven, the earthly fallen,
       rise in it only in sleep
and so on and so forth. i shout loudly because i know

i'm nothing more than a language. i'm allowed to go anywhere
but cannot leave whatever i do.

3. i am the landlord, he says, i live in the attic
and never come down. you couldn't ever have seen me.
'what attic, which attic, we've been living in this room for years,
nobody's ever noticed any attic up above.'
i am the landlord, he says, you can't enter the attic.
'what attic, which attic, this room never had an attic.'
elvira has come in: you men must be blind, the water's already higher than
                our windows.
take your shovels, climb to the attic, thrust them through the eaves, and
                row.
set this ship in motion a little, let's shove off at once.
'but elvira, the landlord's up there, we mustn't.'
to the attic, you wretches, put your hand to the oars, there's no time to
                spare.
'but, elvira, i went up there,' mircea said, 'there's no attic.'
'there is,' i say, 'the landlord's there, the attic's there.'
'there's no damn attic,' he says, 'just a doll on the roof, a broken plaster
                doll,
and a little rain fell last night, elvira,
a few puddles under the windows.
it's always raining through these shoddy ceilings. nobody ever thought to
build a roof up above, an attic.'
and i say, 'the landlord,' and he says, 'just a poor broken doll's up there.
if it keeps raining like this, the plaster will
dissolve before morning.'

4. let him alone, he said, let him be quiet, he can't talk
he's neveropenedhiseyeshasnoideawherewe'retakinghim
sleep, sleep, we won't harm you. don't dig
your nails into your flesh, it's not a shirt, it's your very own flesh.
you can't go out – cover his feet, elvira.

hurry, don't be afraid, we're not taking you far – i wasn't afraid –
don't wake up, she said – i'm not awake. it was
night, it was warm, it was dark. she said damnhe'llneverbecuredofthis,
he'll never understand a thing

hurry, hurry, don't wake up. we'll get home and i'll let you
scratch the plaster of the walls. you can strangle the doll.
you can dig your fingernails into her plaster. but not now. it's still night.
                    elvira,
cover his feet, he's cold.

it was warm. it's cold, she said. it was dark.
if i'd dug my nails into her flesh, i could have gone inside.
she said, don't dig your nails into your flesh, it's not a shirt, it's
your own flesh. you can't take if off.

5. listen and keep quiet: when they carried grandpa to his grave
they dropped the coffin in – not much could be done.
it was as if grandpa wanted in as fast as possible,
as if he were in a big hurry to go down, as if
his body were no more than a thin shirt –
as if he were in a hurry to dress himself in a surer body.

he was in a terrrrible hurry, as if he wanted to throw himself into the grave
as soon as they let the coffin fall. would you like some lemonade?
you're so thin and pale, stop touching yourself, your skin
scratches easily – grandpa was the same.
he seemed to be wearing a shirt instead of a body.

6. (i'm carving a long fingernail. i'm not allowed to have long nails
but i'm carving a fingernail unlike any ever seen before. the walls come
                closing in
day by day, like waves of dough. only the window doesn't
close in. and she moves farther away, she shrinks, she becomes sleepy.
the ceilings come closing in. only the door doesn't close in.
she wrinkles, she dries like a shrivelled mouth stretched over
toothless gums. but i go on carving an incredibly long nail.)

7. she said, elvira, quick, do the shopping, it's already dark.
you won't be back before tomorrow.
they said, he won't live till tomorrow, this one wasn't ready to come out.
his mother gave birth to him before he had a real body.
instead of a body, she must have covered him in a cellophane wrapper –
if he spoke, language would break him.

you can put this one in his grave. he'll believe the earth's
his mother's body. he's better off there.
we'll bring him flowers, really, *we'll* dig his grave, *we'll* bury him –
all you've got to do is keep quiet quiet quiet...
or else he'll go too far, he'll creep inside you as if inside
a mother. he'll break your body trying to get in.

8. (i can hear the walls come closing in day by day. but she
has to be ready by then.
i set her with her root in the earth, i've watered her all the time.
i dug myself a room inside her, round as a yolk.
it will be a fingernail unlike anything ever seen before.
it will grow until it fills the space. dig
itself into the walls. shred the ceilings.
puncture the roof. then it will burst out unforgiving and mute
like a huge plaster doll without a face.)

The Amigo

1. it's rumoured that the amigo, the good buddy came to town.
so people hurry to see for themselves and for a minute we begin to believe
                as well.
but in the square there's only a man more foolish and more down on his
luck than we.
he stands in the middle of the square his hand held out and says he's our
                buddy, the amigo.
everyone standing in line curses him because now, at christmas,
we hoped a different buddy would appear, the true friend.

this guy calls himself the amigo but we know him.
for years and years he's been going around begging in the outlying
                districts.
then he gets drunk and sleeps it off wherever he can lay his head –
he's too much like us to be the true buddy.

but since we're worn out and it's christmas eve and we want to have fun,
we stop, we pretend to listen, we take part in his game
we call him our amigo, since here, on the banks of the
dâmboviţa, we turn into buddies over time, every one of us.

then snow starts to fall, people drift away, we wander back to
our tables in this rundown beer joint.
we no longer hear and no longer want to know anything.
because it's the eve of the holiday that always mocks us.

at about seven he pokes his head in
he's so drunk he can hardly stand and he's bruised all over.
but, since we're worn out and it's christmas eve and we want to have fun,
we shout, come on in, amigo, let's celebrate you.
but now he no longer claims he's the amigo, our true buddy.
he simply asks us to help him keep going,
he whispers he just wants us to lend him a coat, any coat.
go to hell, we haven't got one for you – can't help every damn cripple.
nobody's gonna help us either.

then at the entrance of this dive we notice the cross glaring at him sternly,
staring us down, casting an evil eye.
beat it, we yell at the amigo, get lost,
or we'll all be in bad shit.

when we stagger home, very late, we see him far off, dragging that stick of
wood on his back.
the wood on his back has grown taller than the blocks of flats in long rows.
hell, if we'd believed he was the one, shouldn't we at least have set our
                    shoulders under it for a bit?
but he's too much like us really to have been the amigo,
the good buddy.

2. listen, now, i'm an overcoat, drunk and sick. i'll be damned if anyone
        remembers me.
but once upon a time i fought great battles at thermopylae in the obor
        market.
if i hadn't followed the amigo, i'd have been a doctor's coat or a cop's,
clean, educated, in the lap of luxury.
but since the amigo first put me on, there have been no more good times.
'cause that very day he dragged me to two bars at once.

at first i was disgusted and felt humiliated.
i was hated by those filthy boozers.
then i forgot who i'd been and i drank with him.
i came down in the world. i'd say let's drink, we've
worn this life sometime before, it's already crumpled –
god goofed up and created us again.
four years after that, i didn't give a thought to myself, i could hardly carry
        him to the door.
anyway, the day before whatever it was, i was crushed by tiredness.
he was wearing me, singing and utterly alone. we barely knew how we got
        home.
i can't remember taking him off.
i can't remember falling asleep under the table.
that night he went without me wherever he went.
i swear, i've no idea what happened that night.
i'm an overcoat, sick and old, but an honourable one,
may the devil drag me to hell.

i'm a nothing. a cousin, the amigo's. for three months now
i've made my home in the vasilescus' house.
when i'm with the amigo, i grow important and fill out,
i feel i'm somebody.
but where he suddenly decided to go that night, who knows?
i've no news. he caught me unawares. if i knew he got some money,
i'd say he went back home, to claim his inheritance of laughter
and madness that have been his family's for a hundred years.

3. we too wear the mask of passersby, the amigo says,
and we too are often deceived by them.
we serve them for years and eventually we forget about ourselves.
but suddenly, one fine day, someone knocks at the gate in the evening.
who is it? you ask, since you're one of the victors and nobody
would be looking for you any longer.
wake up, the answer comes, i'm bringing you home from battle,
i carried you on my back all this distance, you've been dead for days.
come on, shall we drink a beer before night falls?
damn it, give me one, or do i have to throw your corpse in the water by
             the wall?

no time to go unlock the door. the man from far-off places has gone on his
             way.
he knocks at other gates, repeats the same words to others –
on a night like this it's not easy to see who's staggering down the road
by himself – maybe you, maybe somebody else.

on the battlefield, the victor goes searching for the defeated among the
             corpses.
come, he begs, it's your turn now to be on top.

4. hey, buddy, if truth still exists, for us
it would be better if it stayed a stranger,
for we're no longer among those who can accept it.
we've sat too long at this table, old habits die hard,
the streets are bustling, our bodies constrain us –
they've always prevented us from being what we wished.
my friend, we no longer drink the way we did last year. we no longer wait
for the one lonelier than we to come and prepare us to save
ourselves. we no longer expect him now.
but we're used to it, and by habit we keep coming
to this table, and if one day suddenly one of us... the others
won't even notice. nobody will
wonder, for nobody here is better than anybody else.
look, pal, we ought to be satisfied with that. so who knows why we're not.
since the father's vanished, anything goes.

5. oh, we're such worthless creatures, worthlessness
itself fails by comparison. we work at it diligently,
year after year, hoping that one day...
oh, we're such worthless creatures, woman who will never be.

nowhere to go. nowhere to escape
unseen, out of this world.
oh, the woman will say, such worthless creatures!
from this moment on, who will...?

6. i am the chair the amigo sat on. i've lived
in the vasilescus' house for eight years. when i was still being made i was
                     told
i wouldn't amount to anything. now i've got to laugh:
i've lived longer than my peers. i've aged rather well.
i've held the whole family between my arms. i've led a useful life.

i am the lamppost by whose side the buddy slept
on the night between the third and fourth of march. i am
the snow he slept in and embraced until he melted me and i was gone.
i was virgin, i'd fallen barely an hour before.
i don't think i'd ever whispered 'my love' to anyone.
i am the streetlight at the crossroads. i stay on all night.
i am the last one who saw him when he went down to the river.
it was after midnight when he passed by me and he was
more a stranger to himself than he'd ever been.

i am grigore, the dâmbovița tadpole, grand duke of sweet waters.
boy, the amigo said, take me across quickly.
aha, i said, that'll cost you, give me a couple of coins and i'll take you with
thanks.
fine, he says, here's a one. i don't believe i'm coming back.
keep the change, put it in the bank.

i liked the guy. on the other side i sent for
the mole to be his guide. she knows every turn and way.
mind you, you good-for-nothing, i told her, don't toy
with this one. i said to him, good-bye, my boy.

i am the mole, my name is mrs cuza. it's my pride
i served the buddy as his guide.
behind us the white world flickered and went dark.

for three days i followed paths known only to me.
nobody ever was above us and it snowed.
on the third day the badger greeted us. he sat in prayer,
his paws clasped and sore. he

was waiting for the amigo. welcome, he said,
i am paul.
the amigo bowed and paul blessed him.

then i don't know how long we walked, except it became darkest night.
a caterpillar in a cassock glimmered among stones.
don't pity me, amigo, here the most humble creature
is dearest to god. i am peter.
my dear fellow, i alone can unlock the gate to heaven over there. first, sit here
with me, and let's chat for an hour.

the garden of heaven covered about four acres
enclosed all around by a wattle fence
and the fields were still unploughed.
do you see, peter asked, the shingled house at the back of the garden? keep
your head bowed, my good man, and betake yourself there. you're expected.
mind you, don't knock on the door loudly, god
may be drowsing or asleep.

the amigo knocked, the door wasn't locked. god didn't hear him
for he was busy throwing a log on the fire.
hi, said the amigo. hi, said god as he hunkered
on a stool by the fireside, warming himself.
god was a runty little guy, mostly bald, cross-eyed,
with a white beard down to his waist.
he spoke teasingly, relaxed,
a bottle on his right, another on his left.
come over here, man, go
roll a cigarette and pour yourself a vodka.
the world becomes something other once you've tossed down a shot.
have a glass, god urged, the way you used to. you used to like it a lot.
no, no, the amigo replied. from now on, god, no.

7. a man alone beside a man alone.
this is how war and peace are ended.

A Life on One Single Day

october 12, 1966

it happened when the ice girl rushed into
the church at seven in the morning. usually we went at
nine. the priest said, what the hell are you looking for
at this hour? you'd best open your ears! the ice girl flung back at him. this
                      autumn
you won't get away with it, the ants have come back to the village. so hurry
                   up,
go home immediately, you're in big trouble.
oh ho, the priest told her, come to me, my dear, let me show you
how potatoes grow under tombstones; someday you'll grow
just like them. and she replied, damn it, don't you know you're defiling
the altar by drinking at five in the morning?
we arrived at nine and the priest greeted us: children, it will be a fine
day today; your hands are blue, which means
all your evil will be lifted off of you. the ice girl
hooted with laughter because under the table the snake
had coiled around the priest's leg. don't let me catch you
playing ball in my garden again, or your parents'
curse will be unloosed upon you. it already has,
the child gheorghe said. what has? the priest asked. last night
a saint stinking with lice came riding a water
horse over the hill, autumn's bound to set on us
very early. the snake uncoiled from the priest's leg
and plopped lazily on the stone floor like a belt.
in the icons a big nobody was painted, a nothing standing on his right.
so, i said, today we've got to bring in the hay
from the far end of the field. the ants have begun to eat it, they'll
swell again if it rains. then instead of oxen
our father will have to yoke a pair of ants to the cart.
get thee hence, the priest said, you little liar, be gone!
the ants only come every seven years, this year isn't when.
ha ha, the priest's black cassock chuckled. hee hee.
heh, the pew guffawed once, gloomily,

they've begun to manufacture the void again at the factory in tismana. you
                little flea-
bitten bastards, you know this is no way to talk. i'll
inform your parents, because wet weather will indeed
come to the village. you stupid priest, you'll be the first
carried away, 'cause you're so impossibly pissy.
the ice girl stood on tiptoe, rose in the air,
flew out the window.
lesson's over, children, the
priest announced, lighting a cigarette.
the snake slithered down between the gravestones, we backed
out, and when we left, there still was drought and night outside.
it could have been about seven. the priest left, too, quite drunk.
under the dome, the ants were eating it away. when they reach the village,
the ants are already enormous. and then it's the year...

october 12, 1976

for four generations, a river of dark
blood has flowed behind our house.
every year, my father covered it with hay and leaves
so our neighbours can't find it. his father covered it with hay and leaves,
        too,
and soon it may be my turn,
since it wouldn't be good for the neighbours to know what's flowing there.

in spring we pretend to plough and sow,
it looks like we're doing what everyone does.
we pretend to harvest in autumn,
trying to appear like everyone else, not get noticed,
but in fact we do nothing but wait, keeping an eye peeled
to see whose turn is next. one of us
surely is next.

we spend our day hating the one who will escape, although
whoever escapes, escapes only till the next time.
meanwhile a current of dark blood
stains the river. we have been covering it with
hay and leaves every year,
since it wouldn't be good for the neighbours to know what's flowing there.
we must appear to be doing what everyone does.

october 12, 1986

from our house, on any given day, the end can be seen clearly.
from the time we were little, we've been told he's one of ours, the im-
poverished landlord whom, out of pity, we've been
hiding in our cellar for generations.
we know exactly what he's going to do when he emerges,
goes up to the house, and claims one of us.

and we know we are lucky!
at least he lets us know beforehand,
we can get ready. we each know
when someone's turn is next.

you, ioan, because you couldn't leave off
drinking, our darling, you'll be picked
very early. remember to say thanks,
for we'll take care of all your expenses.
you've never had a dime, anyway.

october 12, 1963. a tale, home

a ghost owl came in the night and perched on your house.
all heard her shriek *whoo-whoo*, and in one
night the house withered and fell to the ground.
then the ghost owl came and perched in your
apple tree, and instantly the apple tree withered. she came
another night and perched in your
walnut tree. she shrieked *whoo-whoo* and the walnut tree withered.
people began to wonder: how come
the ghost owl sings for you three times this year?
for when the ghost owl sings in a garden,
then, from the garden where she sang, someone's taken away.
you think, this must be an important year for you,
or she wouldn't have sung so often.

october 12, 1989

they gave me this bright-eyed, ready-made
death, so i ran away to bucharest.
it was somebody's turn, i didn't want it to be mine.
maybe that's why they grew terribly angry,
though i'm only thirty-four, since grandpa's
eighty-four already, but he's lost his courage.
that's why they keep telling me to come home.
they've all lost their courage.

in this world that is almost the other,
they secretly want me to be the first, although
one of them's already eighty-four.
that's really why they tell me to come home.
i won't scream, for i'll be wide awake.

october 12, 1988

on wednesday i was alive all day. that seldom happens
to me, and when it does i stay in. then i
have to be wary, lest anyone take note,
for i tend to stagger, and they'll
think i'm going to fall, although
it's the only day when i'm alive.

once a year, on a wednesday, it happens
i'm alive all day long. i don't feel
very good at the time. but i can understand
why everything i love turns against me,
begins suddenly to weaken, hurtle toward extinction,
and turn to ashes.

october 12, 1991

i went back one more time to no. 15 olte☐ street.
i thought i could pray.
over those two years, they'd dragged sacks of plaster into the room.
goddam, don't ask me why, i've no idea what to say.

they made a plaster god as big as a wall.
they tied it with ropes to the ceiling.
what'd'ya think of it, man? they said. see the miracle we made
in our room a year ago.

it was an ugly doll, what the hell – no hands, no feet;
it sort of looked like hans, who always lay dead drunk on the floor.
well, man, they said, d'ya see the god we made?
it's a beaut, isn't it, a god to adore?

come on, i said, that's hans any day.
it's an ass-backwards god, nothing more.

but i was hungry and they said: boy, if you please –
want to be absolved? down on your knees!
cross yourself – then we'll give you cabbage soup with meat.
but if you don't cross yourself, just beat it.
i wept. i crossed myself. i ate. i drank, i laughed.
i left very late, in secret.

october 12, 1990

four men are sitting at a table in silence.
suddenly one starts, comes awake, begins to babble on and on –
among them he's the one whom only the devil himself has heard speak
before today.
he mutters nonsense, says he's
alive, nobody else at this table is alive.
tomorrow morning, no doubt, he'll sober up, he'll
realise how stupid he was.
he won't speak anymore for a long while after that.
the end begins slowly, it looks very much like life.

october 12, 1991

eventually the end comes to me even here where i live.
hey, man, he says, i've nowhere to sleep tonight.
he's stone sober and tells me, it's your
fault i'm sober.
his romanian's a bit shaky.
yeah, i say, ok, i've had buddies sleep here.
but look, as you come in, wipe your boots at the door.
i'm renting this place. you, it seems maybe
you're staying with some aunt somewhere?

no, the end answers, i live with the devil's
dam, way the hell out in the district 'new bucharest.'
you know, i've no winter overcoat, so
i walk around during the day to avoid being asked for my i.d. card.
i go back home at night, totally plastered.

damn it all, god keeps telling me to take you from earth one day,
you'd be better off, no body, no clothes, no need to eat.
but why should i be so stupid as to lose you, sell you out?
now when only you take me in when i've no home,
now when i drink a lot and sing in the street?

october 12, 1992

i am a man alone. no pride in that. lots
of poor s.o.b.'s go about searching for others
unlucky like themselves – but between this yoyo and that
are many degrees of unhappiness.

one's got a lot of money, another nothing more than empty
hopes – only the unfortunate exist,
of every possible sort.

and when, despite all this, they unite,
the poor slobs make revolutions, after which
everything gets taken away from them.

october 12, in days gone by

when i was ten they bought me my first pair of shoes.
they were long, yellow, like coffins.
i never wore them. they punished me
for many years because of this. i've never laughed since.
but my hand began to write.

october 12, 1992

here it's required of you to be afraid, because the strength of the formula
lies in this: your being afraid. that's why

all non-meanings are mobilised. every
meaning is annulled.

you're paid good money to stay where you are and be afraid.
the end begins slowly, it looks very much like life.
you can sit in no place, at no time.
you're paid to be afraid, nothing else.

celestial cars stop in front of your gate at night. you're
taken by surprise and shoved into the vans.
you're not told where to. you're paid to be afraid.
that's why all non-meanings are mobilised.

october 12, 1992

i've returned home after long years of
wandering around bucharest
i've returned with an empty string bag in my hand.
she comes to the gate and says, well,
my dearest, you promised you'd make money.
you said that in two years you'd earn more than others earn in four,
and look, you're bringing back nothing.

listen to me, my dears, i earned nothing.
i'm bringing home more nothing than anyone could
have saved in these two years.
i've hardly been able by myself to carry
all the nothing i've earned.

behind me come carts heaped high with nothing,
near to breaking under the weight.
when all are unloaded in our yard,
nobody will have as much nothing as we.

in a year or two it will be more valuable than gold.
we'll sell it when the price goes sky-high.
my dears, rest assured, nobody has as much nothing.
i've saved it for two years, thinking only of you.

The Banquet

it's always been like this in our house:
three beds that each of us had to cross
in turn. one by one, we went in the same direction
for generations, and over the years it became a law
that stands as the foundation of our home.

we are the last born. the most recently born
are destined to stay in the brightest corner of the room.
we are too fresh in this world to understand
that in this house there also are others. our world
is no bigger than the well lit bed under the window.

a good number of years pass before we realise our parents
live here too, but in another bed, farther on,
where the light reaches with much greater difficulty.
they make much less noise, they move much more slowly than we.
but a good number of years pass before we understand this.

and one day we discover that beyond them, in the darkest
corner of the room, is a third bed,
and when we learn this we no longer laugh.
we thought that there, in the darkness, the world itself ended
but now we find out that someone lives there and nobody
pays him any heed.
i am told, simply, that's the old man of the house, everybody's father.
if there's a father, then that corner is real, i remind myself.
we get used to this and try to forget it. only, at night,
we can hear from the old man in the corner a hideous gasping –
why the hell is he sleeping in the room with us?

i am still in my bed under the window but i no longer laugh
at the man who gasps in the opposite corner.
i believe deep inside me that someone wants us not to see.
when one day he is carried out, he disappears from the room
shadow and all, to us he will remain a great unknown.

i'm allowed only to touch the new wood of the coffin.

next my father goes from the second bed,
shadow and all, to the bed now empty.
i take his bed, and younger flesh occupies my former bed.

it all happens slowly. each of us goes from
bed to bed in turn after a long wait. one wins
one's next bed after a fierce battle,
a long, secret struggle.

those in the first bed long for the second, it can be
seen in their eyes. at night i myself
feel a strong impatience to take the place
of the one in the third bed, the man who gasps
more and more hideously in his dark corner.

then one day the third bed is again empty, the one
from there carried out and packed into a fourth bed
that has a lid so he cannot somehow come back, because
his bed has already been occupied, and others have rushed to the second
                    bed,
and the new guests in the first bed cannot hear yet
that someone already is starting to gasp in the bed way back there. that
                    someone is me.

and at that moment the day turns brighter.

SELECTED POEMS 1996–2009

i don't know why father yoked the oxen to the cart

i don't know why father yoked the oxen to the cart
at midnight, woke me, and said let's get going –
after i die i can finally sleep a deep sleep. where? i asked,
and he replied, to big şomcuta. what did he want
in the middle of the night at big şomcuta,
such a long way from our village? why not take
the bus at six in the morning? why should we journey
four hours there, four hours back
at the slow heavy pace of our oxen?
no, when it comes to such folly, you won't catch me home any time soon.
i just won't get up in the dead of night to do something crazy like this.

and then she approaches my bed and says, wake up,
mama's dearest, your father's
already on his way to fetch you from şomcuta.
go help him lift you up, for
you've been lying there three days with no living breath.
the news reached us only last night,
our darling boy.

across the road from the pub where i sit drinking

across the road from the pub where i sit drinking,
there's a church. the priest and i have watched each other for years.
i'd like to serve god too but i'm afraid.
he'd like to have a drink with me but he doesn't dare.

he raises the cross at me in a rage
and threatens me while i raise my mug
of beer at him and threaten him.
i stamp my feet with fury and he's angry, too,
he shakes his fist and stamps his feet behind the window.

maybe i shouldn't come for a beer on sunday
as early as seven in the morning. he begins the service
at nine. but at seven, precisely at seven,
he sneaks in the altar and we begin to gesture at each other.

we watch each other constantly for two hours. when the service begins
he's never himself; to those around him he speaks
confusing words, raises his voice, forgets his sermon, interrupts what he's
                    preaching,
and the whole time he runs again and again to the altar,
lifts the curtains, looks for me, dances a little jig,
shakes his cross at me like a raving madman.

he threatens, almost breaks the windows, and i get even more
furious and raise
my beer mug higher. so he runs back and talks to
the faithful. he doesn't resist for long, though, he rattles through
his sermon at breakneck speed, he can't wait to get rid of
the congregation early so he can return to the window.
likely his sermon talks about me and my sin.
just as in the pub i keep telling everyone about him.
all those like me who live ass backwards forgotten by fate

will one day enter the church heads bowed,
and the priest will forgive us and bless us.

then we'll throw a party in your honour, father.
i'll foot the bill for everything. you can drink in peace, we won't
have anyone to tell. then we'll go drink more at your house,
it'll be late sunday night, nobody can see.
just stop threatening me. i'm already scared to death
of those who threaten me with eternal life, father.

at thirty-six i learned to pray. it took a lot of effort but i managed

at thirty-six i learned to pray. it took a lot of effort but i managed
to get a god of my own, a rubber doll dressed in rags,
with thick lips, an arm detached at the shoulder,
its rubber belly gashed open. in the end,
only this much divinity was mine to know.
it's likely this rubber doll isn't the worst god
ever vouchsafed to man.

here, in the room where i stay, i put him in the place of honour, on the
                table.
i'm not ashamed to pray to my god, this sort of god,
after i stagger back home drunk, hardly capable of hurling
two or three shameless words at him before i collapse,
head on the table, hand at his throat.

it's true, with this rubber god there can be little forgiveness.
all the same, crippled as he is, he looks much less indifferent.
when i pray i don't yell. why should i? he can't hear anyway.
yet i cut off his ear so it would seem to me
that if i'd left it, he could have heard. so when i pray
i don't yell. i never complain. never beg for mercy. i've learned to pray
to all worthless things. i no longer look toward heaven,
it's all too clear: that's not where i came from.

i pray as i can: sometimes lying on the floor, other times
hissing an obscene song in his good ear,
he can't hear anyway, but with him there's less fear,
less loneliness in this house.

surely my death will turn out as pitiless for me
as the death the others' god prepares
for each of them according to their lot.
but my god i can forgive for that, as well.

he hasn't any idea. he sleeps toppled over to one side on the table.
i don't yell when i pray. he can't hear anyway.
i slowly hum a ribald ditty, i lurch at him, grab at his throat,
stumble, fall to my knees.

job. iova. jonah. ioan.

in the beginning was the end. then the agony. then the dry land.
then on november 16 i saw iova walking head down
at the intersection of victoria and lemnea. it was a friday night.
now, please listen to me: i had no money and wanted to forget. i caught up
        with iova,
asked for some money. iova didn't say anything.
it seems he was in the middle of a divorce or something, for he suddenly
      took
his crown of thorns in one hand and flung it down as if it were a cap.
what are you doing? i asked him. the owl said, let him be,
and landed on top of his head, croaking.
let him be. resignation is
his nickname.

i've had an ultrasound, iova said. i'm
the tenant of a grave. they saw it inside me very plainly.
never mind, i said, they'll manage somehow to remove it. don't fret –
they have forceps, they have catgut, they know their job.
come on, relax, give me a cigarette.

damn, the grave keeps growing bigger every day, he says. it's begun to
      press on the lungs
and now it's reached the liver.
then, i say, let's go to this bar here, 'the ram',
we'll fill it up so you can have a sea in that dry land.

not now, iova says, i haven't written in months. i'm no longer
waiting for anyone from 'the megara'.
when i write, the paper's too thin and it shreds.
look at this: i'm wearing gloves so no one can see, because now
i write directly on my hand: this is my late aunt.
i write hard. i push the pencil point into the skin until
i find myself under it. i write as deep down as i need to dig in.
i scratch tissues, i rake veins, i gouge bone until i hear
the graphite pierce the coffin.

i incise a letter a day. enough until i find myself. the rest
is silence. no other writing is comparable to this. then,
until the skin heals over, i write on my palm, i write on the back.
that's why my wife left me: writing's too full of pain.

i write until the letter sinks into flesh. one day i'll be read
only on the inside. i'll be a book bound in my own skin.
inscrutable. when they open me on one half,
i'll turn to my other. i'll stay
inside forever. they'll search. i'll laugh.

so come on, old man, now let's go to 'the megara' or 'the ram'.
today's our last chance, since tomorrow
will never be tomorrow.

the city

'what unexpected opportunity for war, this peace,' the first-time visitor to our city tells himself. a woman has recently brought a child into the world. for this she will be punished according to our local laws, because, our laws hold, yet another life brings after it yet another death. the more lives, the more death. but here we're always vigilant to reduce the quantity of death by reducing the quantity of life. only the one who no longer has anything is worshiped in our city, since possessions increase the wish to be, the thirst for life, and consequently fear of the end and of endlessness. however, our laws aren't yet strong enough to put a stop to all births. through the mother's transgression, the newborn will be mourned for months, and the mother must bear two unending guilts: life will grow in her immeasurably, and death will grow in her to the same degree. life never forgives life.

the city laws say the past must constantly be burnt to ashes, but this isn't so as to enhance the future, merely to restrict it to today. too much future arouses expectations that give rise to forbidden vital fevers. closing off the future means making death and fear of death bearable: a life lived at a low flame means a death decreased by half.

people nobody knows come to this city a couple of times a year – bodies full of themselves, boisterous natures, infuriatingly alive. they talk about their fortunes, about love and hate, tomorrow and yesterday. we scorn them the most and pity them, for they've not yet known nothingness. after a month or two, when they leave, they've already begun to show a face something like our, and our idols', wax faces, the immobile beauty of statues. some of them give up all they had and had been, in deciding to stay. here, the past never hurts and the future never brings defeat. because those who are the defeated have conquered the sickness of being the conqueror.

you must not boast that you are. to be means to live a life, a much more hazardous fortune than that of things that can be seen. when our dead die, they are not very dead, because they don't depart from a full life, but rather one that seems fraught with shadow. our living aren't very much alive, as from childhood on we help them to bear only as much life as can end in untroubled death.

at four years old i aged overnight, in order to be like the true citizens of this city. since then i've remained unchanged. he who obeys laws learns that the truest truth is untruth. for this, feasts are laid to which nobody comes to celebrate the one who will never be. we prize only that which grows dark, decays, and approaches sunset. all that is born and lives to the utmost exhausts us.

i have seen young people sneak away from our city for places where life is in full bloom. they spend two or three years there, they begin to hope and to feel despair, to cultivate life and celebrate it, to strive after riches, to love and to hate. after a while, everything there turns against them.

most of them come back and once again start over here, fervently practising the exercise of ageing. in the end, they become the most obedient to our city laws. but whatever they tried hard to partake of in these other places leaves on their faces a suffering never to fade for however many years they have left. those who fail to come back, i'm told, never learn to cope with foreign cities. soon they are shoved aside, pushed to the outskirts. they return to worshipping our wax-faced idols.

a man was caught last night who secretly drew the earth swollen with vegetation, naked women dancing, tables laden with wine. he will be taken to the public square and judged for these monstrous forms of imaginary life he intended to sell on the black market to others as sinful and sick as he. he will be locked among creatures with a full life; he will tear himself to pieces within a few months, because there, in the reservation where we send those brimming with life, no city dweller holds out for long. he will be badgered to come alive like the others but doesn't have a quarter of their power to live. he will get thrust forcibly out of their lives. next, death will grow quickly inside him, as big as the life he craved. our laws always bring justice, and our wax-faced idols protect their true subjects.

religion in our city is diminution and disintegration. from the time we're little, we're taught to wipe out in us all that soars, all that longs to pervert with too much life. we work toward the worthy objective of failure and mediocrity, and our visionaries are convinced that, once we shrink enough inside, death shall at last have no dominion over us. we will float infinitesimally close to it, infinitely far in time, without ever falling definitively into it. that will come to pass only because, in the here and now, we will have made a good beginning. because we have managed to reverse the sign of unhappiness and misfortune, to turn them to our advantage. emptiness, mistrust, helplessness have become steps in the growth of our diminution. thus we pass through an initiation: from disappointment to misfortune, then further, to helplessness and indifference, then to untruth. and this becomes the truest truth. the ultimate step – the highest or lowest. it is the union of nobody and nothing as one in the deepest depths.

in our city, time is no longer measured, for nobody perceives it any longer. hence, a multitude of non-existences have become material, real, undeniable. we are very nearly nothing and no one. nobody and nothing acquire visible existences, as palpable as we who dwell in this city. death, on the other hand, shrinks to a domestic trifle. in the flesh of an ever more clearly revealed nothingness, all our gods can be seen reconceived. seeing nothing, we can now see our gods. at present, they remain half asleep, hazy, tremulous shapes, but when we come to tread upon nothingness as firmly as we tread upon the ground of our city, the gods will reunite with us, they will clothe us anew.

at four years old i aged overnight. now, in this book, my work speaks volumes about the diligence with which i have studied so that i might become a true citizen of our city. i soon anticipate a darkness more blinding than daylight. a deafening speechlessness. what unexpected opportunity for war, this peace.

there's not a lot of death on tuesdays here

there's not a lot of death on tuesdays here,
but not a lot of life either. phoenicians bear gifts
that few can buy.

it's like that until our earth-dwellers
are told the tale of the lives of their sea-dwellers.
at that moment, our humans start to dream
of buying sea and selling land.

it's no accident that the phoenicians vanished
to ply the dry land instead.
it's no accident that our humans vanish
to buy the sea from phoenicians.

nobody seems to care: a gradual somnolence
envelops our world and the next.
nobody remembers anyone as if
each of us had been in his grave forever.

once a month, once a year, someone comes, his shadow
looms over the edge, and we think it's god.
but it's an ominous, silent shadow that can do no better
than heap another night on this night down below.

with these eyes that i've never seen with

with these eyes that i've never seen with
more than a meter away,
i smell light as if something strange
and in the process of vanishing,
flesh on flesh in flesh under flesh,
and i think only now have my eyes begun to see it clearly

as at last it assumes its proper form,
a paste denser than metal, heavier than water –
otherwise how could it sink to such depths?

but what eye purer than mine can see light in its essence,
its dark veins ready to burst,
more disturbing than a placenta in the garbage,
heavier than quicksilver when it labours in birth,
and, when it sees so much, what eye bustles every
which way, as if around a cauldron of asphalt?

with an eye like mine you can't see light radiating,
instead you see its sick substance,
its weight more massive than darkness.
only the feeble, half-blind eye can see the light
that's invisible,
the light that rots in the yards on sundays,
too weary to fade completely.

the bristly, short-sighted eye flow after it
sees what eyesight has never seen,
that matter itself isn't heavy, just the light pressing upon it.
only eyes that go bad can see that.
whoever sees only light sees nothing at all.

but whoever doesn't see it collects it in large barrels
over which he places burdock and stones,

he stores it for years until it settles to the bottom,
hardened like mastic.
one day, in astronomers' telescopes,
it will look like a thick, dark oil
he will use to anoint his body.

maybe then the eye, that always
hinders sight, will wither away.
when he sees with his skin, man will no longer be man,
and the religion of the retina will have died.
god, as long as he exists, cannot withstand sight,
but then he cannot escape us.

he becomes part of the light that
the ordinary eye fails to see,
only my almost blind eye.
from the light above, things become heavier and heavier
and once you ascend there's no return –
the heaviest weight is weightlessness.
when you ascend you become the massiveness of that other world,
you plunge into invisibility like a sack of stones.

man is heavy in the other world
because of light: the light of veins,
the great carpathians of light in the sternum,
the sombre lights inflating his bones.
who said man isn't light?
in the invisible, man becomes light itself,
a clot of deathly ill lights.

few will be the things
we fail to see because of light,
but because light never helps sight,
and anyway my sight is weak,
between my blinders
i at once see light without light.

and when the flesh goes blind, my eyes will see
the fleshly light that causes us to putrefy.

if i hadn't been forced to start talking

if i hadn't been forced to start talking,
i'd never have spoken a word.
before i turned six they never insisted,
which was good. i stayed beneath speech
as if under a hermetically sealed cast-iron bell.

i was hiding a knowledge
that they forced me to lose when i turned six.
i could see the angel not in sleep but for real,
in broad daylight
when reality can't be denied.

i never forgave that they
sent me to school
where i was forced to talk,
and later i had to try and be like
the others, who talked fast
and moved their arms and legs,
confusing me with their lives.

even today i talk only with fear
because i still live there, under the bell,
and speech is bad for me.
i have nothing to say in human speech,
which is all about hubbub and happenstance.

with a certain cunning, however, i pretend
to talk, they can hear
almost human sounds on the outside,
but in my throat vibrates a shapeless, illiterate moo
that has nothing to do with words.
even worse, the knowledge of my own secret speech is gone,
gone, too, the angel who for six years kept watch
at the head of my bed,

gone, too, the man who could have been a different person
always silent in this manner until at the end
of many mute years he would reveal
the least forgiving of all knowledge,
the only knowledge that might have made death more bearable
and machines kinder.

in early spring, people sleep longer

in early spring, people sleep longer.
after so much winter, calcium has leached from the bones;
wars can't start then.
warriors are asleep with exhaustion.

not before april can they undertake
a new campaign to increase the number of the dead.
otherwise, why would they fight?

it's no different at the black sea,
although wars no longer last sixty years.
even though spring arrived
quite early and people
have awakened before their time,

their weapons are rusty, and those who are up
have no idea whom to aim at:
a great silence reigns.
you shouldn't start a war unless you know
which side will lose.

when i was a small child, i dreamt of being even smaller

when i was a small child, i dreamt of being even smaller,
smaller than my father's big boots.
no bigger than a potato is how i dreamt of myself.
because in spring they put po-
tatoes in the ground, and that's it,
they never bother about them till autumn.

i dreamt of curling up in a hole among them,
sleeping sweetly in the dark,
turning to one side and the other all summer long,
then falling asleep once again.

in autumn i awaken still unrested,
unwashed like my brothers,
and when the spade thrusts near i leap out
and shout: stop digging, stop digging,
i'll gladly come back home
if in spring you return me here.

so in spring i'm the first
they drop down into the hole.
in this way i could go on sleeping forever:
from the ground to the cellar, from the cellar to the ground,
year after year, undisturbed and forgotten.

beyond

it's been nearly twenty years since beyond went away. a little before and then during my time, beyond was the only place that really existed, the only place worth living for. beyond was food and drink to us, hearth and home. incredible things were said about it. it worked inside us with terrible power. it made possible the day still to come, although that day was the same as yesterday, the same as tomorrow.

vienna, budapest, belgrade... everything came from beyond and everything happened beyond. when nothing seemed possible any longer, beyond was the only possible thing, although no one had ever actually run across it. love lived beyond. fortune lived beyond. hope lived beyond. god lived beyond.

then suddenly beyond was right here. but when we reached beyond, we found out it was not what we had been dreaming of. ten years later, when no more was said about beyond, we in fact understood the farther we advanced beyond, the farther away beyond became. it was no longer in vienna, neither in budapest nor belgrade, not even in london or paris.

now i know: if we keep on longing for it with all our might, we will have to go beyond beyond, so far beyond that no trace of here would be left. could we reach it by train? never. by ocean liner? no, no matter how many seas we crossed. by airplane? not even if we travelled a thousand years without a stopover. in its own unique way, however, beyond seems somewhere near us, very near. it just doesn't move in our direction.

The Author

Ioan Es. Pop was born March 27, 1958, in the village of Vărai, Maramureş, a province in the north of Romania. Upon graduation from the University of Baia Mare in 1983 with a degree in Romanian literature and language, he was assigned to teach in the village of Ieud, where he stayed for six years and which became the punning name of the mythical locale of his first poetry collection. *No Way Out of Hadesburg* (in Romanian, *Ieudul fără ieşire*) appeared in Bucharest in 1994 and was immediately recognised as a major book. Reviewers and critics have praised Pop, 'one of those rare *poètes maudits*,' as 'the most profound... lyric voice of the '90s generation of poets' and characterised his work as 'bizarre and deeply tragic' and 'eloquent.' The Romanian Writers' Union awarded Pop its prize for a first book. Meanwhile, Pop had moved to Bucharest in 1989 as a manual labourer. After the Romanian revolution, from 1990 on, he worked in journalism, as a proofreader and, ultimately, editor. Today, he is editor-in-chief of *The Sunday Paper* (*Ziarul de duminică*), the cultural supplement of *The Financial Daily* (*Ziarul Financiar*), and also senior editor of the review, *Discovery* (*Descoperă*).

A second volume of poetry, *Porky* (*Porcec*, 1996), soon followed his first, then a book of poems with his Bucharest address as its title, *No. 113-bis Pantelimon Highway* (*Pantelimon 113 bis*, 1999), which won prizes from both the Romanian Academy and Writers' Union. Four years later, Pop published *Party on the Crosswalk* (*Petrecere de pietoni*, 2003), which was awarded prizes from the Writers' Union and the rival Association of Professional Writers of Romania. In 2004 Pop was granted the honorific Order of Merit from the Ministry of Culture. His other books include bilingual collections published in Romania, *Rugăciunea de antracit/The Anthracite Prayer* (2002) and *Lumile livide/The Livid Worlds*, (2004), both with English translations by Nathaniel Smith, K. Shaver, and Ion Creţu; a pair of volumes of selected poems, the more recent entitled in English, *No Exit* (2007); and joint volumes with other poets. Currently Pop is working on a new collection of poetry to be called *Tools for Sleep* (*Unelte de dormit*), likely for 2011 publication.

No Way Out of Hadesburg is his first book in English to be published outside Romania.

The Translators

Adam J. Sorkin most recently published *Memory Glyphs*, a collection of three Romanian prose poets, Cristian Popescu, Iustin Panța and Radu Andriescu (Twisted Spoon, 2009), and Ruxandra Cesereanu's *Crusader-Woman*, translated mainly with Cesereanu (Black Widow, 2008), and he is the main translator (with the poet) of *Rock and Dew: Selected Poems* by Carmen Firan (The Sheep Meadow Press, 2010). Other publications include Radu Andriescu's *The Catalan Within* (Longleaf Press, 2007), translated with Andriescu; Magda Cârneci's *Chaosmos*, with Cârneci (White Pine Press, 2006); and Mariana Marin's *Paper Children*, with various collaborators (Ugly Duckling Presse, 2006). Sorkin's awards number among them the *International Quarterly* Crossing Boundaries Award and the Kenneth Rexroth Memorial Translation Prize, as well as arts grants and publication support from the National Endowment for the Arts (USA), Rockefeller Foundation, Academy of American Poets, Arts Council of England, New York State Arts Council, Romanian Cultural Institute, and Fulbright, Soros and Witter Bynner Foundations. His Bloodaxe books, Liliana Ursu's The *Sky Behind the Forest* (1997), translated with Ursu and Tess Gallagher, and Ioana Ieronim's *The Triumph of the Water Witch* (2000), translated with Ieronim, were shortlisted for the Weidenfeld Prize. He teaches at Penn State Brandywine, where he holds the title of Distinguished Professor of English.

Lidia Vianu, a poet, novelist, critic, and translator, is Professor of Contemporary British Literature at the University of Bucharest, where she is also Director of CTITC (Centre for the Translation and Interpretation of the *Contemporary Text*) and editor of the online publishing press *Contemporary Literature Press* (http://mttlc.ro/editura) and the online review, *Translation Café* (http://revista.mttlc.ro). She has been a Fulbright lecturer at the University of California Berkeley and SUNY Binghamton. Her literary criticism includes, *The Desperado Age: British Literature at the Start of the Third Millennium* (2004); *Alan Brownjohn and the Desperado Age* (2003); *British Desperadoes at the Turn of the Millennium* (1999); as well as *T. S. Eliot: An Author for All Seasons*. She has also published two books of interviews, *Censorship in Romania* (Central European University Press, 1997) and *Desperado Essay-Interviews* (Bucharest University Press, 2006); a novel, *Prisoner in the Mirror* (1993); three poetry collections, *1, 2, 3* (1997), *Moderato 7* (1998), *Very* (2001); English learning manuals; and five edited anthologies. This is her sixteenth book of translation.

Sorkin and Vianu won the Poetry Society's 2005 Corneliu M. Popescu Prize for European Poetry Translation for Marin Sorescu's *The Bridge* (Bloodaxe, 2004). Their translation of Mircea Ivănescu's *lines poems poetry* appeared from University of Plymouth Press in 2009.

Acknowledgments

Grateful acknowledge is made to the editors of the following journals where these poems have previously appeared, sometimes in slightly different versions:

The Bitter Oleander, Poetry International Weblog, Words Without Borders.

The translators wish to indicate their gratitude to Institutul Cultural Român (Romanian Cultural Institute), Bucharest, for its support of the publication of this book.

Hardback edition first published in the United Kingdom in 2010 by University of Plymouth Press, Scott Building, Drake Circus, Plymouth, Devon, PL4 8AA, United Kingdom.

ISBN 978-1-84102-209-3

A CIP catalogue record of this book is available from the British Library

Series Editor: Anthony Caleshu
Translation: Adam J. Sorkin and Lidia Vianu
Publisher: Paul Honeywill
Publishing Assistant: Victoria Halliday
Series Art Director: Sarah Chapman
Consulting Editor: Liz Wells

Typeset by University of Plymouth in Janson 10/14pt
Printed and bound by R. Booth Limited, Penryn, Cornwall

Visit www.uppress.co.uk/romanian.htm to learn more about this series

Published with the support of the Romanian Cultural Institute

20 Romanian Writers
2009 - 2013

Publications November 2009

Occurrence in the Immediate Unreality
Max Blecher

ISBN 978-1-84102-207-9 Hardback

This autobiographical fiction offers an intimate and unsettling account of Blecher's ideas of self-identity and the body. He explores the 'crisis of unreality' in relation to the human condition and shares his adolescent experiences of physical infirmity, social isolation and sexual awakening.

Six Maladies of the Contemporary Spirit
Constantin Noica

Posthumously awarded the Herder Prize, 1988
ISBN 978-1-84102-203-1 Hardback

In this unique work, Noica analyses history, culture and the individual in what he describes as the fundamental precariousness of being. 'Maladies' of the spirit are no longer debilitating, but creative for our European interest in change, unity, and diversity.

The Cinematography Caravan
Ioan Groşan

Romanian Writers' Union, Prize for Prose, 1992
ISBN 978-1-84102-205-5 Hardback

A black comedy set in 1960s Romania: a Stalinist propaganda film truck rumbles into a forgotten village in Transylvania. The occupants of the village believe in the traditional values of church and God and are in no mood to participate, placing obstacles in the way of the Cinematography Caravan. However they soon realise the best way to deal with the representative of the communist party and these films is to cooperate.

Lines Poems Poetry
Mircea Ivănescu

Botoşani Mihai Eminescu National Poetry Prize, 1999
ISBN 978-1-84102-217-8 Hardback

Ivănescu's poetry represents the achievement of a little known master. Centring on a wide cast of characters including his alter ego 'mopete', Ivănescu's idiosyncratic, lyrical sensibility offers allusive, comic and elegiac meditations on our common lot.

November 2010

No Way Out of Hadesburg and other Poems
Ioan Es. Pop

Romanian Order of Cultural Merit, 2004
ISBN 978-1-84102-209-3 Hardback

Originally a teacher in a village here called Hadesburg, Ioan Es. Pop
expresses in his poetry his response to existence in Romania under
communist control, forbidden to write but able to work as a builder on
Ceauşescu's palace and living alone in a bachelor block. Pop's poetry
is an autobiographical account of such a time, a life with no way out.
The world of the poems is a closed, boundless imaginary space, charged
with dramatic intensity and tempered by a bittersweet, compassionate
existential angst.

Who Won the World War of Religions?
Daniel Bănulescu

City of Munster European Poetry Prize, 2005
ISBN 978-1-84102-212-3 Hardback

Contemporary madness in its entirety is summarised in Daniel
Bănulescu's play, set in an asylum populated with twelve dangerous
madmen who are divided as believers of the four major religions. This
is theatre in a world governed by insanity; as Dan Stanca remarks, the
play could be set anywhere - in Piteşti, in the Siberian Gulag, in a Nazi
concentration camp, Maoist or Khmer Rouge extermination camp, and,
even, in one of the CIA's secret prisons? This is the principal merit and
black humour of the play.

The Băiut Alley Lads
Filip and Matei Florian

România Literară and Anonimul Foundation Prize for Debut Novel,
2004
ISBN 978-1-84102-219-2 Hardback

Following his prize-winning debut novel, Florian leaves the Romanian
village life behind and takes us to Băiut Alley in Bucharest.

Two brothers, Filip and Matei, are growing up in a totalitarian society.
Every day life is recounted through their young eyes. Their story is one
of childish naïvety set against a backdrop of life imposed by communism.
Their world is filled with characters from children's television, broadcast
by the official communist media, alongside magazines and cinema. 'Joe
Lemonade', 'Giani Morandi', 'Rome Specs' and 'Brooslee' accentuate
the absurdity and grotesqueness of their surroundings.

The brothers become close through a shared love of football,
supporting the same team, Dinamo Bucureşti. Ultimately, *The Băiut
Alley Lads* is a novel about miracles that take place within a nightmare,
regardless of whether they occur in an obscure lane in an obscure district
of a country kept in obscurity by communist dictatorship.

Auntie Varvara's Client
Stelian Tănase

Awarded a Fulbright Scholarship, 1997
ISBN 978-1-84102-221-5 Hardback

The pre-communist nickname for the Siguranţă (Romanian Security
Service) was "Auntie Varvara", and so communist underground members
are literally "Auntie Varvara's clients" of the title.

Stelian Tănase explores Romania's communist 'roots of disaster'
from early illegal membership of the communist underground to their
eventual rise to power and the struggle for supremacy. Tănase sketches
a pattern of warring factions through an incredible swarm of characters
who abruptly fall completely silent after the final victory of Gheorghiu-
Dej and the formation of the communist police state and its hierarchy. A
Romania then on course for human disaster.

November 2011

Dazzler
Mircea Cărtărescu

Grand Officer of the Cultural Merit Order, awarded by the Romanian
Presidency, 2006
ISBN 978-1-84102-206-2 Hardback

The first book in the Dazzler Trilogy describes a communist Bucharest
awash with thrills and nightmares. Dazzler opens with a sixties bedroom
view obscured by towering prefab blocks - a Romania in rupture. His
writing is influenced by childhood memories; hearing the screams of
political prisoners being interrogated and only now revisiting these
places as they are gradually torn down. The essence of Cărtărescu is to
capture the socialist capital leading up to the moment of its downfall.

Wasted Morning
Gabriela Adamesteanu

Romanian Writers' Union Prize for the Novel, 1983
ISBN 978-1-84102-211-6 Hardback

Wasted Morning is a truly modern novel, beginning and ending in the
present yet resurrecting a Romania of the past. The story centres on
Madam Vica Delcă who visits Ivona Scarlat. During this visit Ivona
receives news of her husband's sudden death, triggering memories of the
past which are then re-lived. Adamesteanu creates a world of old upper
bourgeois Romania at the brink of World War One.

Small Changes in Attitude
Răzvan Petrescu

Grand Prize at the 1st Edition of the Camil Petrescu National Dramaturgic Competition; Romanian Writers' Union Prize for Theatre, 1995
ISBN 978-1-84102-214-7 Hardback

Răzvan Petrescu is cited by Adriana Bittel as one of Romania's finest short prose writers. This anthology of short fiction paints each story as a photographic reality and journeys from realistic black humour to the ironic and fantastic. This collection includes his 1989 debut, 'Summer Garden', 'Eclipse', a modern take on the biblical story of Cain and Abel, and 'Friday Afternoon' wherein an epidemic kills everyone in an apartment block. The title truly summarises this anthology; Petrescu suggests small changes in attitude.

The Book of Winter
Ion Mureşan

Romanian Writers' Union Prize for Poetry, 1993
ISBN 978-1-84102-213-0 Hardback

There is both an enigmatic and an original character to the poetic language of Ion Mureşan who concerns himself with the political nature of Romanian poetry in this anthology. Mureşan's poetry draws upon Transylvanian legends to address the communist manipulation and monopoly of truth by regaining individual thought through his poetry, which reflects upon what it is to be Romanian.

November 2012

Silent Escape and Impossible Escape
Lena Constante

Romanian Academy, Lucain Blaga Prize, 1993
ISBN 978-1-84102-216-1 Hardback

Lena Constante is one of the few women political prisoners to have written about her years of imprisonment. She describes in detail her physical and psychological humiliation and suffering in the solitary confinement common in communist Romania. The whole premise of this novel rests on Constante's ability to survive, to escape into her mind and on solidarity with other female inmates. A work of human survival against the odds.

French Themes
Nicolae Manolescu

Romanian Ambassador for UNESCO, 2006
Romanian Academy Member, 2007
ISBN 978-1-84102-208-6 Hardback

Inspired by the combination of political intrigue and love contained within the belles lettres of the great French novelists, Manolescu uses this recipe to tell the story of a great love. Cristina Chevereşan considers French Themes as "love declared or merely suggested, patient and durable, arousing the aromas of French perfumes but also a reading in culture and civilization".

The Iceberg of Modern Poetry
Gheorghe Crăciun

ASPRO Prize for the Year's Best Book of Criticism 1997, 2002
ISBN 978-1-84102-204-8 Hardback

Gheorghe Crăciun redefines modernist poetry through the analysis of Wordsworth and Coleridge, Baudelaire and Whitman. Through this Crăciun proposes a new direction for modern poetry, one that is in permanent tension. This eventually leads Crăciun to consider a third direction, one that revisits old traditions that are still reflected and reinflected in modern poetry. *The Iceberg of Modern Poetry* is a 500 page authoritative contribution to international debate on this subject.

Picturesque and Melancholy
Andrei Pleşu

Ordre national de la Légion d'Honneur, to the rank of Commandeur, and then Grand Officier, 1999
ISBN 978-1-84102-218-5 Hardback

Pleşu questions European culture through the aesthetic of melancholy and literary picturesque myths of Western culture. A controversial text at the time it was written, he approaches the topic from a philosophical stance with an exuberant writing style and an undertow of the subversive. He fell out of favour with the communist regime and was banned from publishing which resulted in his exile to Tescani a community in Bacau, Moldova, Romania.

November 2013

Diary of Happiness
Nicolae Steinhardt

ISBN 978-1-84102-210-9 Hardback

Romania was not the place for a Jewish intellectual at a time when the regime was re-Stalinising. Steinhardt could have escaped prison if he became a witness for the prosecution in a communist show trial. He refused and was imprisoned in 1959 for 'high treason' and 'machinating against the socialist order'. These pages are an introspective diary of Steinhardt's prison years, as Romanian literary critic Mircea Martin explains, *Diary of Happiness* is not only a revelation of faith, but is also a revelation of freedom and of inner freedom.

The Children's Crusade
Florina Ilis

România Literară and Anonimul Foundation Prize for Book of the Year, 2005
ISBN 978-1-84102-220-8 Hardback

A train is hijacked by children, who organise resistance against the authorities sent from Bucharest. In their attempts to negotiate, the authorities prove hypocritical, lacking any understanding of the children's demands. The novel presents a clash of ideologies relating to what it is to be Romanian and to the realities of life under Ceauşescu's communist rule. Ilis weaves two differing viewpoints together, reversing perspectives and constructing a world adrift.

Little Fingers
Filip Florian

România Literară and Anonimul Foundation Prize for Debut Novel, 2004
ISBN 978-1-84102-219-2 Hardback

Florin takes the reader to a small Romanian mountain village near the ruins of an old Roman fort where a mass grave has been discovered; are these remains medieval or modern? A human atrocity, but is it best to ignore, or confront, the past, any past? Whether ancient, or from the recent past, the grave brings back memories of all that is tragic in the former Ceauşescu's communist Romania. Many characters propel the story forward: the arrival of Argentinean forensic investigators, the priest Onufrie, and, of course, the mystery of missing finger bones, which disappear from the pit each night.

This title within the 20 Romanian Writers series is subject to change with another Filip Florian publication.

Cioran Naive and Sentimental
Ion Vartic

Romanian Writers' Union Prize, Cluj branch award, essay, 2004
ISBN 978-1-84102-222-2 Hardback

A biography of Emil Cioran, a philosopher and freethinker, born in Transylvania, who had an inferiority complex and was ashamed of his birthplace. Cioran was attracted to Western culture, because his perception was that Eastern European countries have always been dominated by Western European history. Vartic suggests that Cioran represents one extreme and that Romanians are proud of their cultural heritage, taking the virtues of home and making it theirs.